The Trump in You.

Acting like Trump is actually a good thing.

Bryan Crabtree

TALK40.com BOOKS

For more information on this book or other publications please email editor@talk40.com.

FIRST EDITION

Cover design by Stewart Williams/Reedsy.

Cover photo: Donald Trump speaking with supporters at a campaign rally at the Prescott Valley Event Center in Prescott Valley, Arizona by Gage Skidmore.

Copy editing completed by Daniel McCurry.

ISBN: 1986219585
ISBN-13: 978-1986219587

DEDICATION

This book is dedicated to my wife, my soulmate and my best friend,
Mackenzie. I love you.

CONTENTS

<u>INTRODUCTION</u>

When I pick up a book, I like to begin with chapter one and start reading the subject. Therefore, I'm not going to bore you with a long introduction. As you'll learn later in this book, "less is more."

I wrote this book for one reason.

My goal is to explain why the most successful people are usually the most controversial and why the world wants you to believe that people like Donald Trump are wrong.

This book is not about selling you on conservative policy, Trump policy, or even the qualities of Trump as a person. This book is about selling you on you. This book is about the propensity to be consumed by others and distracted from your own potential.

You may want to live your life in peace avoiding conflict, disruption, and activism, but you'll regret it in the end. At that point, it will be too late to salvage your lost opportunities and your squandered purpose here on Earth.

Like him or not, Trump will not question whether he gave his best effort or not at the end of his life. Will you?

This book is not promoting abusive behavior. It's defending against it. This book is not about how to get rich. It's about how to have wild success and enjoy the benefits of a full life. I hope this book helps you find balance and purpose.

I've experienced wild success and catastrophic failure in my life and I will teach you how to realize the former while avoiding the latter.

I will give you plenty of personal stories so you can understand why I'm more than qualified to enlighten you on this subject. Most importantly, we'll reflect on the qualities of Donald John Trump, the 45th president of the United States and why everyone has the ability to tap into their potential.

Most of Trump's 'qualities' have been decried as liabilities. He's been described as a misogynist, racist, xenophobic, bigot, unpresidential, and unbecoming with a lengthy list of negative adjectives.

Losers define successful people who are candid and ambitious in these ways to explain why they are failing or simply not reaching their potential. Moreover, losers define others this way in order to insulate themselves from the emotional pain of realizing their views are fundamentally out of touch or just plain wrong.

Regardless of whether you are a Trump supporter or not, he has brought to light some of the existential cultural and security threats of our time in a way no president since Reagan has dared to tackle. He has sparked a debate that has awoken America to its political and cultural demise. His election has created division and political chaos, which is forcing us to have a discussion about solutions we have been avoiding.

He has tapped into the hearts and minds of millions of Americans who feel rejected, forgotten and, frankly, weird because our society has dismissed their right to feel or speak a certain way. He has told them that they are not alone.

No matter how he did it, what he said, or what he believes, this very successful American has done something that most people never develop the courage to do. He reached inside his heart and mind and found his most core convictions and presented them to voters.

 He became the 45th president by being transparent about his feelings and beliefs. Trump's entire life has been a series of successes that resulted from not allowing the world around him to control his destiny, purpose, or direction. He's anything but perfect, but no American is 'better' than him even if many on cable television and the political elites act as though they are.

 I'm about to explain how you can realize the purpose in your life and the success you deserve by rejecting the sentiments of the world around you, their demands of you, and their efforts to limit and define you.

 You're about to have your own Trump revolution, that is, unless you're 'too good for that.'

CHAPTER ONE
Integrity

President Trump is one of the most misunderstood people in American history. The irony in that statement is that he understands himself better than most Americans even understand themselves.

In this book, we are going to explore the traits that every person possesses (including you!) that can make you an exceptional and transformative leader and help realize a level of success you never thought possible.

Trump knows who he is and he's unwavering and unwilling to change, regardless of how powerful the outside influences and forces are suggesting he do otherwise.

I call that integrity.

Even if you are completely opposed to Trump's policies and agenda, don't be clouded by your own emotions and don't deny yourself the opportunity to understand the "Trump in You."

Before we dive into to the "Trump in You," let me give you a little personal background so you can understand the perspective of this book.

I grew up in a very stable household in what I would call a "reasonably privileged American family." We didn't have a lot of money, but it certainly wasn't the super challenging 'real world' that many people face. We were candid with each other in a very Christian home. My extended family had very little controversy. It was a simple life, but I always wanted something far more stimulating.

By the time I was twenty, I had worked at a couple of the top music-radio stations in America.

I had become an emotional train wreck after years of experiencing the pressure of 'real' society and attempting to portray an image that wasn't really true. It was a false image that would net acceptance, advance my career, and would attract more people who would like me (we'll cover being liked in a later chapter). This false image/ life would never earn me the respect and dignity that every American wishes to achieve.

After years of being someone other than myself, I was riddled with anxiety, bouts of depression, and self-doubt.

I was young. I was alone, and I was miserable. I woke up to the fact that I had to make significant changes in my life one day while living in Montgomery, Alabama. I was working in country music radio and beginning to realize ratings success. In a short time, I had achieved the number one rating on the station even though some of our staff were market veterans. I wasn't failing. I was just on a path to winning by being a fraud - someone other than who I was really destined to be.

Literally sitting in the fetal position in the middle of my tiny, home studio, I decided I had to leave Montgomery and fast.

I didn't know it at the time but God was about to put me on a path I could have never planned for myself. Within days, I landed a job as the morning host of a country station in Huntsville, Alabama.

What I didn't know was that the program director who hired me was forced to do so by the station owner. My boss ultimately wanted the job he had given me for himself. At twenty years old, I was about to learn a brutal lesson about company politics. Every attempt to be a more genuine person was met with ridicule and unfair criticism. Society pressures us back into compliance unless we build the strength and fortitude to push back and endure the pain.

After several months, I simply couldn't take it anymore and moved back home with my parents. I worked in Nashville radio part-time and hosted a syndicated Sunday night show on a Christian radio network for a few months before landing a job in Memphis, Tennessee at a country music station as their creative services director.

I had grown substantially as a person and had learned to be more transparent and more genuine. But, something was still missing. I was consumed with image and how other people perceived me.

This consumption can become a sickness that causes you to do the exact opposite of what's in your best interest. You become a toxic employee, acting with destructive insubordination and unwittingly undermining the agenda and goals of the company.

Psychologically, it's a self-protection mechanism. When you're not living as your true self you become a leech that sucks the energy out of other people. Deep inside, I realized I was flawed. Our self-protection and self-esteem frequently allow us to bury the harsh realities we must face in order to succeed and fulfill our purpose.

Lacking the deep connections that every human needs, we seek attention in any way we can find it. Under these circumstances, it usually requires being an incredibly negative and unwelcoming person focused on the wrong things which ultimately sucks the energy out of everyone around you.

The next time you meet someone who is dreadful and negative, just remember this person is likely attempting to gain attention and seek connection with others. They are just doing it all wrong.

In my own story, I was on a path to being fired but I didn't know it. By this point, I had been at three different companies in a single year. The same person kept showing up at each of these three jobs destroying my success. I couldn't escape that person no matter how hard I tried because it was me.

But, again, God had a different plan for me when I boarded a flight from Memphis to Charleston, South Carolina in March of 1998.

In Charleston, I sat at a bar with a program director who was about to launch a country music station for a small broadcaster. It was an instant friendship. We had a lot in common including similar personalities.

He was several years older than me, unmarried, and without children. He lived a fun life and he had a great job. At times, it was like I was looking into a crystal ball as to what my life would be like if I stayed on that path: lonely, mildly successful, and looking for far more out of life as it 'passes me by.'

I knew something was wrong and I knew it was nothing outside of me. I started this chapter by telling you in not so many words that I had a 'near perfect' childhood. It was about as perfect as you could hope. But it also set me up for failure by not dosing me with the reality of what the world is like: strife, divorce, violence, drugs, discrimination, and disappointment. I could depend on my family at all times, but I never knew this side of life until it was dealt to me.

If I had stayed in my hometown, like most of my family and childhood friends, I may have lived a peaceful simple life, but never experienced the world as it really is. Many of my former classmates tell me today that they feel trapped and nothing around them seems to have changed. They decry the fact they still go to the same places, doing almost the same things as they did in high school. I see both the positive and the negative in that even if they don't.

The world is a cut-throat place full of frauds, criminals, losers, and bad actors. I believe everyone is born innocent and with a good heart. The world corrupts all of us in some way. The world had corrupted me. I wasn't a criminal. I simply wasn't on a path to realizing my full potential and instead was on a path to becoming stuck, resentful, and regretful.

I was a chameleon, only interested in the next big opportunity and didn't care who I stomped on or plowed over to get there. As a result, the person I hated most was myself.

As an on-air country music disc-jockey, it would be an understatement to say that the people who we the 'talent' most disliked were the sales staff.

They're the lifeblood of any organization but they were my archenemies in Memphis.

I found out from a friend after I left Memphis for Charleston, that I had been just a few weeks away from being fired as a result of my attitude with the sales staff. It wasn't that they didn't deserve it. It was simply that I wasn't empowered to be the person holding them accountable and I was extremely arrogant to think that was my role.

That was about to change in Charleston. I sensed that if I partnered with these new salespeople and did the exact opposite of what failed me in Memphis, I could actually turn them into my biggest advocates. By attempting to build genuine relationships with them and make their jobs easier that would make my career path more tolerable and maybe even enjoyable.

I was still miserable because I didn't understand why I had so much anxiety. I was getting better but I was still portraying a fraudulent image.

Looking back, I was only 21 years old. That's no excuse. We are who we are and we'll never change that. Society unwittingly tells us that being genuine is somehow unacceptable and weird. The best hope for anyone is that they can understand who they are, accept it, and own it.

I was lucky in Charleston. The sales manager was supposed to be the person I could never tolerate, especially as an on-air talent. But we found a connection. Growing up in Tennessee, I have always been a Volunteers football fan, and so was he. He brought me to the local 'Tennessee Vols' Alumni club and I watched our team win a National Championship that year.

I have a love for sports mainly because it's the one thing that can bind people from all backgrounds and demographics that otherwise have nothing in common.

Over those months, I went to NASCAR games with my boss, football games with the sales manager, and as a result befriended everyone in the sales department. I had the exact opposite experience of what I had created for myself in Memphis.

But, oddly, I was even more miserable because now I had to face the fact that I had damaged myself for years and was horrified that I might do it again. Like many Americans, I literally didn't trust myself.

During this time of personal crisis, we grew the radio station from number 14 in the market to number 4 in just six months. We tripled the revenue and I was offered a job programming a heritage country station in Columbus, Georgia.

They begged me to stay in Charleston and I did. It would turn out to be the linchpin that would shape the rest of my life…. until now.

Shortly after I signed a new contract, the station in Charleston was sold and brought under new management. With it, we had despicable nepotism and an unintentional sabotage at a level I've never seen since.

I was now riddled with anxiety, fear, and a new bout of quasi-depression. I had made a horrible calculation to stay knowing the company was about to go through a transition.

After the program director, my immediate boss, was fired, I put up a valiant effort to get his job. I deserved it. It was a team effort, but everyone knew I had been a powerful force in getting earned media and growing the listenership of that station by partnering with our promotions team. My guerrilla-marketing had been laser focused and extremely disruptive to our main competitor. We had them chasing us at every event, on-air promotion, and imaging opportunity. We were winning, but the ratings just didn't fully reflect that yet.

I had earned the position of my former boss, but there was no chance they were awarding it to me. I now admit I was not ready in terms of maturity to lead a staff of a dozen people. The vice-president of programming told me "sometimes you have to move out of the company in order to prove yourself and move up in the company." That was a punch in the gut.

It was the turning point in my life. It was the moment that I stopped trying to be someone other than who I really was. It was the moment I took off the gloves, stopped walking on eggshells, and simply jumped without a parachute. I knew the plane was going down even though no one else could.

At the time, there was a huge real estate boom in Charleston where home prices had risen 20% or 30% every year. I had more appreciation in the prior year on my small home in Goose Creek, South Carolina than I had earned working 60-70 hours per week for a $35,000 salary. I decided to get a real estate license and start investing in real estate.

 Over the next several months I would flip my first home, make about $20,000, and close my first deal as a real estate broker. For some reason, I was really good at real estate sales. By September of 2000, I had several clients looking for homes and a couple of closings pending.

 The new general manager of the radio station, in an effort to give his trophy girlfriend a job which she couldn't earn herself, decided to start cutting salaries, including mine. I looked at him and told him that I considered that a termination and that I was rejecting his offer for a new position. He was stunned. This was the moment where I came alive and realized what I would later describe as the 'Trump in Me.'

 This book will take my experiences and attitudes that have sometimes seemed weird, combative, irresponsible, or unprofessional and explain why they are anything but. We will fully explore President Trump's campaign for the presidency and help you realize exactly why the things that caused him the most grief were the very things that validated him the most. You will see clearly how the things we most avoid in life are sometimes the most beneficial. In a small way, I've lived a similar personal revolution and can see it in a way that almost no one in the media can.

A few months before that 'ass-wipe' general manager decided to take part of my salary to give to his 'gold-digger of the month' I had begun taking control of my own destiny so that I would never again have to depend on someone else for my livelihood. Why would anyone do that?

It's perfectly fine to have a job earning a salaried income, but you better find something else to build wealth!

I looked at the general manager and said "I believe the legal word here is a constructive discharge which is the same as firing me from the contract." Shockingly he was unaware of the terms of the contract I had with the company, which required them to pay me several months of severance and they did in one fat check.

This loser barely made it a year at the company before they fired his ass. The station saw its ratings collapse and never recovered again. The powerful sales staff fled and the revenue was destroyed. Later, the signal was moved out of the market to Columbia, South Carolina.

The next year I made $250,000 in income, going from $35k to $250k in one year. At that point, it wasn't about the money. It was about proving that the real version of me could take me beyond the limits of imagination. I was pissed. I had worked 60-70 hours per week for this company, helped build a solid radio station, and they dismissed me like yesterday's burrito after my morning cup of coffee!

My next personal challenge was about to develop.

In direct or indirect ways the people around me, likely threatened by my talents, always tried to keep me in a box. They offered unending and unsolicited advice. In life most of these people do not have your best interests and successful future in mind. Their advice is centered solely on what's best for them even if they don't realize that's what they're doing.

No one in your life can advise you on what decision to make about your life or your career. Stop asking for help making the decisions that shape your future. Ask for help on individual components of it, but not its totality.

The more successful I became in the real estate business, the more I realized that all of the people who were judging me, bashing me, and attempting to compete with me were simply helping me. They were essentially reminding me that I had to keep proving that being genuine and transparent was the way to free myself from what most Americans never escape from: a lackluster life, especially in their career, where they never break free to realize their true potential and purpose in life.

The only difference between you and our president Donald Trump is style. You may not speak the way he speaks. You may not think the way he thinks. You may not believe in the things he believes. But you have the capacity to be a billionaire or a millionaire or president (of something) if that's what you want.

Every time the media reminded voters that Trump had no political experience, had filed business bankruptcies, failed at his vodka venture, or didn't pay a small-town contractor (because the work was shoddy), they thought they were serving to defeat him. Trump was a major threat to the political establishment and media. I was laughing the entire election season because I knew from my own personal experience every time they made fun of him for being an American dreamer; they were unknowingly offending and poking fun at their audience. Trump knew he could manipulate this.

 The takeaway is that he did exactly the opposite of what the media and political class expected because he could predict their reaction each time and knew it would validate that he is an outsider who would go to Washington, kick ass, and take no prisoners. Average American voters had been waiting for that for the last three decades.

 I have to give a disclaimer. Not everyone wants to miss their children growing up, go through two toxic and expensive divorces, and face the volatility of business bankruptcies and public embarrassment in order to achieve what Trump has achieved. That was his choice. It shouldn't necessarily be yours.

 We all have different purposes and expectations of life. For some of us, it's helping a few families in our community. It could be as simple as changing generational poverty or a few families' legacies of criminality. For others it may be helping young children find a better path instead of the one for which they're destined.

Some people dream even bigger. For others, their passion could include becoming the congressman for their district, making a product that solves a problem for thousands or even millions of people, or building a company that can be passed on to generations of descendants that creates a better life and legacy for their family.

You have to know what you want your life to look like when it's over before you can have the life you deserve and desire on Earth.

News flash: it's not about stuff, money, or prestige.

One of the biggest misconceptions about President Trump is that he lives his life for the purpose of money or attention. The losers call him a narcissist, a man with dementia, or a psychopath. These pundits are so arrogant (and have been for so long) they stopped learning decades ago. Complex people like President Trump overwhelm their intelligence and psyche. They choose to dismiss complicated people like him to avoid confronting their own weaknesses. Trump's statements often challenge their world view and even values (which are derived from years of avoidance of reality). Additionally, they simply lack the cognition to understand they are projecting their own worst traits on others.

People who obtain success at the highest levels never get there because they want the money. They find something they deeply love, overcome incredible difficulties (when most people would give up), and become an expert at it. At the onset, they're normally faced with naysayers who say "you'll never be successful and you'll regret the direction you're going".

When President Trump was in his twenties, he wanted to build skyscrapers in Manhattan. Many think this is just part of his narcissism, as they call it. It's not. We all have a deep conviction in our core about who we are and what we feel called to do. We mostly ignore those passions and convictions. He didn't. That's about the only real meaningful difference between Trump and you.

He recognized an opportunity to do something in Manhattan that other people weren't doing. He looked at the most brutal, expensive, and difficult real estate market in the world and found something that everyone else was missing.

Success is about finding what an entire culture or industry of people are missing or not doing and connecting that to the sentiments of how people perceive that part of culture or industry.

People are so negatively affected by Trump's transparent and genuine demeanor, no matter how toxic they believe it to be, that they miss the formula to his success. The example I outlined above is a simplistic example of his formula and style that works.

In being offended by Trump, people frequently miss the 'hard-knocks' he faced and the humility of sidelining his dream in order to learn how to succeed.

Trump didn't start in Manhattan; he just knew that's where he was called to be. Trump's first independent real estate deal was in Cincinnati, Ohio. He had many other deals along the way that were outside of Manhattan. For years, he did projects and managed buildings that were anything but who Trump is today. For lack of a better way to describe it, they were "low-end" real estate.

That was all about to change in 1978.

CHAPTER TWO
Break Free and Find the 'Trump in You'

Donald J. Trump's first real Manhattan estate deal was the revitalization of the Grand Hyatt next to Grand Central Terminal. Obviously, Trump had learned the art of 'location, location, location' early in his real estate career.

The idea of tackling this project was met with ridicule and the sentiment that he was guaranteed to fail - by nearly everyone around him. He shut off and shut down those voices and simply didn't listen to people telling him he couldn't be who he knew he was called to be.

For lack of a better way to say it, "he didn't give a damn what you think."

Over 80% of what our population believes about any particular subject is either skewed or wrong. This develops from overthinking a subject, leaning excessively on the opinions of others, or seeking media that validates your wishes instead of reality. Odds are your gut feeling, the first time you contemplate a subject, issue or challenge, is what's best for you. Trust your gut and you'll find the 'Trump in You.' Even if you fail, you'll learn how not to make that mistake again.

Trump started the Grand Hyatt deal in 1978 and by 1980 had completed it. Next he was moving on to develop the iconic Trump Plaza.

Let me give you an insight into loser mentality. If your reaction to what I just told you is that "I can't do that because I wasn't born with a silver spoon in my mouth," you're already well on your way to failure. Everyone explains away another person's wild success by finding a perceived disadvantage they personally have in accomplishing a similar goal.

It's true that Trump got his first $1,000,000 loan from his father Fred Trump. His father was a silent partner and he convinced a bank and the government to back the $70 million loan needed for the Grand Hyatt. Did his father help him? Yes. But the point here is that Trump pursued his dream and leaned on the resources around him to help him get there. "No" was not an option.

For you, it's important to identify the resources around you. You can't measure your success and potential by comparing it to someone else's.

Based on the arbitrary and unilateral standards created by the Washington, DC establishment and its media bubble there was "simply zero chance this man could be the 45th president of the United States." However, he did what we've already established is also the secret to **your** success. He didn't listen to the world telling him what he couldn't do.

 He did it anyway and instead manipulated such ignorant sentiment and statements to serve as his advantage. Most media "experts" still don't realize what happened to them and how he used them for victory. They were and are too arrogant.

It's a certain path to failure if you listen to defeatist voices.

 It's estimated that Fred Trump had a net worth of $250 million at his death. As part of the Grand Hyatt deal Fred Trump gave his son $1 million in cash as a loan and partnered in the guarantee of the $70 Million construction loan. That means he risked nearly 30% of his net worth as a bet on his son's potential.

The average American family has a net worth of approximately $500,000 at retirement. Think about your parents. Imagine that's how much they have in total net worth. Now imagine that you approach them at dinner and ask them to pledge

$150,000 of their retirement savings and net worth for a business deal you believe with great passion you must do.

What percentage of Americans parents would do that deal? There's simply no way in hell many would do that deal.

However, for the extremely small segment of the population that's graduated from a top business school with honors (Donald Trump from the Wharton School), worked for the family (Fred Trump's) business with a great deal of success for years, independently found success on smaller projects of their own, doesn't have a drug or alcohol problem, and displays incredible discipline, their chances are significant. Trump was forced to earn the right to tap into 'daddy's fortune' and that was perhaps more difficult for him than what most of us face because Fred Trump's standards were extremely high.

The point here as that the losers dismiss Trump's success as being a product of being born into a wealthy family when in fact it may have presented a much bigger obstacle for him than most. Most rich kids feel entitled to the money; Trump wasn't.

All that money growing up as the son of Fred Trump wasn't an advantage, it was a disadvantage.

It may have expedited Trump's financial success but it created a rigid, disciplined, and powerful businessman, destined for greatness that would create an imbalance in his personal life.

In other words, Trump made a choice. He was absent as a spouse, a father, and a friend but laser focused and extremely present as a businessman. Any accomplished businessperson would seize on that and partner with a guy like Trump, especially his father.

This book is a formula to find the Trump in you through self-reflection, not the formula to become a multi-billionaire like Trump. This is about being the real you, not being a fraudulent version of Trump. Don't let the title misguide you.

The only thing you need to find when you finish reading this book is your purpose in life - the one thing that will give you more reward than anything else. The rest of this narrative is about teaching you how to ignore the toxic and demonic forces of our troubled world that plan to stop you at all costs.

CHAPTER THREE
The Troubled and Demonic Forces of #Nevertrump

From a 30,000 foot view, when Trump came down the escalator in 2015 and announced his run for president, it appeared that everyone was against him.

Unbeknownst to 'everyone,' Trump had been listening to everyone. At a recent one-on-one lunch, one of his top campaign officials told me that Trump had been listening to talk radio for the year prior to his historic escalator ride. He wasn't listening to radio hosts and talking heads like me; he was listening to the callers: YOU.

 These are the people, now staunch Trump supporters, that had been forgotten, diminished, and even abused by the powerful elites of our society. He heard what they said, their passions, and what they wanted done. It was a chorus of like-kind thought that seemed to be a billboard that told him specifically what to do should he run.

 Ironically, regardless of his past politics, what they were saying aligned with what he had been saying for 30 years. It was common sense.

Common sense and logic are very offensive because they ignore how language makes others feel. Be willing to offend others with the truth if you want to be successful.

These were things like "our leaders are letting us get taken advantage of." He would say "we are acting as the world's police, we are losing our sovereignty with porous borders and we have people who don't understand business running our government."

Remember, these "people" are the people that judge people like you and Trump with their useless textbook mentality. They believe that in order to be the president, you have to 'check certain boxes.' It's a type of bureaucratic test they personally write to try and trick you while maintaining their superiority over you. They believe that being able to regurgitate textbook material is more important than your ability to lead and execute your vision.

Academic achievement does not display the capability of anyone, especially you. Some of the most accomplished people in academia also are the most incompetent in life.

While completing a college degree or attending a top school is a significant achievement, it does not insure success. You must also be able to make sound judgments and execute while using your knowledge.

 I graduated from high school with 3.8 GPA (number 12 out of 250 students) and earned several scholarships for academics and leadership. I tell you this to build a foundation for this statement: Most of the tests I've ever taken to reach those achievements were written by stupid people who had no idea how what they 'know' applies in the world where you have to 'do' in order to succeed. How could they? They sit in an office and figure out how to indoctrinate the rest of us.

 For some reason, I rejected the concept of school from the age of five and I've never changed. I don't give a damn if my kids go to college or not. College is a rite of passage in some careers. I'm in the business of thinking and speaking. Why do I need some professor who has never run a business or really done anything telling me how to think or speak? To hell with that!

 For a lot of these 'expert, highly intelligent' professors, their finances are a mess. Their relationships are even worse and most of their business endeavors (if they've ever tried) are miserable failures.

That's why it was academia that first pointed out the failures Trump had experienced in his life. Again, we call that "PROJECTION."

Idiotic people, especially if they see you as a threat, will find your weak moments in an attempt to diminish and define you. They have to because most of the acumen and intelligence they have portrayed is fraudulent. These idiots are fear mongers and they project their own weaknesses onto their opponents to prevent being exposed for their true intentions and behavior. They have to distract from the fact that they have always been called the smartest people in the room but in fact may be the dumbest.

A large portion of the army of #NeverTrumpers is made up of people that don't really know how to do anything because they never have tried. They are intellectually lazy. They are people who never break free of the chains and the fraudulent version of themselves that I described at the beginning of this book. Their entire life is one misrepresentation after the other, and they never disrupt it to find out who they really are.

Deep down they know it, but the thought of coming to grips with decades of their destructive, self-defeating behavior is so emotionally devastating they choose the easy route of projecting their weaknesses on people like Trump.

Never forget what I'm about to tell you. Most of what we despise about other people is also what we despise the most about ourselves. We're just usually unwilling to admit it.

When someone makes you angry, in most cases, the anger stems from seeing a trait that subconsciously you dislike about yourself. Think about that the next time you get angry, and it may begin to change your life.

The people saying that Trump has dementia or emotional problems or painting him as a bigot, racist, or xenophobic are projecting their own traits on him. That's why his statements are contorted and twisted into being much worse than they are and why the 'offended' are so passionate. They are subconsciously upset that he is initiating a conversation they wish to avoid out of guilt or fear of finding out they have been wrong.

If you believe those things about Trump but aren't possessed by proving them, you certainly have that right. I'm not suggesting you are wrong because you disagree with Trump's positions, but the act of constantly shouting from the rooftops the same insane accusations with the hope that you will change the direction or stop someone (over which you have no real power) is the reality of being the very person that troubles you the most.

Trump refused to apologize for being who he was even though these people and the media demanded it constantly. This brings us to our next point about finding the 'Trump in You.'

Stop the damn apology tour in your life!

CHAPTER FOUR
The Apology Tour

This title may sound like a departure or distraction about the Obama years. It's not. This chapter is about exactly what it says: "the apology tour."

At some point in our lives, we all go on an apology tour.

Stop doing that! You are destroying your success, your credibility, and your life. Apologies are weaknesses resulting from being unable to explain or take corrective actions.

I must apologize, in advance, for shifting this example as a reflection on President Obama, but I'm going to explain why, by giving you background on this phrase.

Okay, I'm really not sorry and I shouldn't have apologized, because I'm going to talk about Obama anyway. Do you see my point?

The term 'apology tour' was made popular in the first year of the Obama administration as he toured the world as our newly elected president. It was clear that he was apologizing for our past behavior he believed was unbecoming to the

United States. He felt that we were, at times, bullies to other countries and cultures.

 I'm not inclined to disagree that there is some truth to that sentiment. However, he wasn't elected to be the 'apologizer in chief.' He was elected to lead America in a positive direction. Apologies are a sign of weakness, a mistake, or failure. Having to make an apology is a direct admission of failure. In apologizing for some of our terrorist driven wars, he failed to admit the legitimate reasons we did that. He completely dishonored the fight to rid the world of terrorist cells.

 He toured the world (early in his presidency) decrying our capitalist economy, seemingly promoting the socialism of Europe as a better alternative. Europe has moved toward a more socialist and destructive political scene that ultimately reduces the human condition and diminishes individual rewards for success. We shouldn't apologize for drifting away from such nonsense.

 The disaster for Obama's legacy is that this country mandated (through the election of Trump) the virtual destruction of all of his policies. This is very sad even if you disagree with them. Obama achieved the most powerful position ever known and because of his loser mentality riddled with apologies, his legacy is being destroyed. Obama did that, not anyone else.

Obama apologized for mistakes made by the CIA as they were desperate after 9/11 to keep more innocent Americans from being killed by evil terrorists. He apologized for the war on terror that we engaged in to destroy the cells of evil that populated war torn countries. He apologized for America getting "off-track" even though we are still the most philanthropic and strongest proponent of democracy and generally improving the human condition in the world. Why apologize for something for which you are still the leader? Here's the answer:

People who apologize are all weak. But, more importantly, they are seeking to steal approval in an instant instead of earning it over the course of time.

Being liked by other people is one of the most overrated emotions/goals in our lives. Being respected is the Holy Grail. What this means is that anyone can be a chameleon and achieve likability. As much as I despise the policies of Obama and his administration I have to admit he's a likable person. The problem is that I have no respect for him. In my view, he only achieved one thing while president of the United States. He did something of which we should all be proud. He came from humble beginnings as an African-American and became the first black president in our history. His election showed the possibility and capability of the experiment called the United States. It showed our greatness in terms of how we can evolve, change, revolutionize, and accomplish things that seem impossible previously. Even two decades ago, it seemed unfathomable that a black man could ever be president.

His election showed how America can evolve and improve yet his first act was to apologize for the country that made him a key benchmark of American greatness.

As with most professors/academics Obama failed at everything else. Trump went from nothing to attempting to build a skyscraper in Manhattan. Remember, he did many small projects and paid his dues for years prior to his first big deal in Manhattan. He had to prove himself before 'daddy' would give him the first loan.

I sincerely believe that Obama's policies and legislative efforts reflect his deep convictions. The fact that I vehemently disagree with almost all them is irrelevant here. In the long term, he accomplished almost nothing. He saw leadership as management instead of making and forcing change and he squandered his potential to affect change and his life's purpose by doing it before he was prepared.

Leadership is setting a goal, executing a plan, and insuring that it will endure far after you are no longer involved. Management is directing the staff to put new price tags on the clothes at Walmart for the 'back to school' sale. Obama led his White House as though he was a department manager at Walmart. He didn't create lasting change. Instead, he made sure everything stayed the same, and in most cases, became worse.

By contrast, Trump has been talking about running for president for the last three decades. Trump was never known to be one to apologize, partly because he rarely did things that distorted who he really is. Living a transparent life, even if you unintentionally cause damage, is never bad (so long as you right your wrongs immediately).

A 'demanded apology,' especially in politics, is an attempt to change someone's values and convictions live and in the public square. To apologize for something you said in a moment of passion is to deny that such beliefs existed inside of you.

Trump took a lot of heat for saying "he preferred war heroes that didn't get captured" in reference to Senator and war hero John McCain (R-AZ), who was a prisoner of war for five years during Vietnam. Trump had waded into a subject that was culturally considered taboo and would do nothing but destroy his political credibility. It didn't, because he didn't apologize. In essence, he spoke to a crowd of people who believed with conviction that John McCain was a curmudgeon, who made everything in his life, including his service to his country, about himself.

This book is not identifying whether that is true or not. This book is about finding deep connection to people who are central to your success by saying things to them you're 'not supposed to say' except that you believe and feel that it's right.

Trump did things that were uncharacteristic of any presidential candidate before him. He called Texas Senator Ted Cruz, "Lying Ted." He called his Democrat opponent Hillary Clinton, "Crooked Hillary." Trump even attacked a Gold Star dad who accused him of not understanding the

Constitution. This was "certain to end his presidential bid," according to the media, and everyone demanded an apology. Instead, he doubled down on his conviction and ultimately exposed, Khizer Kahn, the Gold Star Dad, as an immigration lawyer from New York who preyed on loopholes in our immigration policies. We discovered that this Gold Star dad would lose business if Trump was elected president. It wasn't about 'America,' for the Gold Star dad, it was about money.

By apologizing and kowtowing to the elites/experts for his supposed wrongdoing, Trump would have unwittingly admitted that he been wrong and Kahn was right. Instead, we learned that Kahn's only goal was to make money without regard for the damage it caused to our society. There will be more discussion of these campaign 'greatest hits' near the end of this book.

Let me say this again: stop apologizing!

There is one exception to this rule. When the Access Hollywood tape was released in October 2016, and we heard candidate Trump asserting that his celebrity gave him the right to "grab women by the pussy," he did apologize. He had no choice. There was no chance of him being elected president if he did not set the record straight and tell the American people that he felt that such rhetoric was inappropriate and unbecoming. Many have challenged the sincerity of the apology, because so many are disingenuous. I believe this one is different.

 At times we say things we believe or think are appropriate for that setting. Obviously, Trump wrongly believed his "grab women by the pussy" comment was fitting on the Access Hollywood bus. My point here is that he thought it was clever and funny at the time.

However, the election was over 10 years later and it is certainly acceptable to evolve in your thinking. It is my belief that the reception he received from the evangelical community (during the election), his age, and newfound presidential-purpose challenged him to change. He realized that while he thought it was cool on the Access Hollywood bus, it was now disruptive to his plan. If you think my assessment of this issue is too generous, just remember, this is his only apology during the campaign. When someone rarely or never apologies, I tend to give them the benefit of the doubt and believe them when they finally do apologize.

When someone consistently refuses to apologize every time someone demands it and then suddenly they do, the apology becomes incredibly believable. It says to me they're embarrassed or horrified by the behavior they've displayed as they recognize that most of us find it despicable. None of us should be in the business of judging other people. That is one of our greatest flaws when we do. I can respect the apology, whether I believe it or not, because he consistently refused to apologize just because one was demanded.

In essence, Trump's apology, regarding despicable and vile comments, added integrity because he hasn't spent his lifetime apologizing for who he is. It said, he would apologize when he feels he is wrong or knows that others collectively believe he is wrong. We had been told and convinced that he was so arrogant that he felt he was never wrong. Most of us believed that. So, when he apologized, it actually helped him in my opinion. The worst moment of his political career resulted in it being the biggest moment of growth for his campaign - as bizarre as that may seem.

Throughout my life, my aggressive actions have created conflict, disruptions, breakdowns in relationships, and have likely distanced a number of people from me. Excellent! Revealing to the world who I really am attracts some people and distances others. Why is that bad? I'm ridding my life of the people that limit my potential and the accomplishment of my purpose.

I remember a real estate agent in Charleston, South Carolina who once said back to me "God dammit Bryan! Nobody ever stands up to you because they're afraid of you and I'm going to do it now and I'm not putting up with you. You're not gonna bully me." She was upset at me because I put a very nasty, Trump-like post on Facebook regarding her behavior from the prior day and called her by name.

She had requested an appointment to take her clients inside the home that they were buying for an inspection. We already had it under contract with her clients. It was a high-end home owned by a prominent doctor with a very busy life and schedule. She demanded aggressively that I make the inspection happen at a specific time. She called multiple times demanding an answer and confirmation. My client was in surgery most of the day and didn't get home until late that night.

She was abusive of my time and of my clients' personal privacy. I sent a text-message, left a voicemail, and sent an email demanding she not go to the home the next day until I got back to her with approval. She went anyway, early in the morning and woke my clients with two men walking on their roof. My clients freaked out. I came unglued because of the outright insolence, lack of respect, and lack of regard for personal privacy. I was stunned by this display of ego and disrespectfulness in defiance of someone's personal property.

Being a radio host and a consumer advocate, I turned it into a story about how I felt real estate agents are some of the most disrespectful people in American business. I named her. I called her out. Apparently, no one in her life had ever had the balls to make her look in a mirror and feel some sense of accountability for her egregious, disrespectful, and horrific behavior.

What she had done was clearly illegal, a licensure violation, and could have resulted in someone being shot or killed.

What came next were threats of lawsuits, ethics complaints, and personal attacks - AGAINST ME. The moment you stand up to someone who is accustomed to plowing over everyone else in their life, you will be met with the harshest of reactions and threats. The most common threat to speaking your mind and being truthful is a reaction by others threatening a lawsuit. By finding the 'Trump in You,' lawsuits no longer scare you.

Lawsuits only scare people who are not sure if their convictions and actions are appropriate. Most people have learned to address the threats against them by bullying you and beating you into submission. The request for an apology is usually the first step followed by a threat similar to a lawsuit or ethics complaint (such as in real estate). Most of the time these threats are not followed by action. These losers typically crash and burn as fast as they erupted because they know they have no righteousness in their outrage.

I'm not saying you'll never be sued by standing strong for your convictions. But, it's much more rare than you think.

My scenario I just described, to many outsiders, was explained by calling me a loose cannon or "that's just Bryan and "his angry reactions to anyone who dare stand up to him." Now, connect this situation to Trump early in the campaign, as he took out nearly 20 accomplished political opponents one-by-one to earn the nomination.

Millions and millions of Americans in the media completely misunderstood just how calculated President Trump is in every response, counterpunch, tweet, and statement. He's not a loose cannon at all. Every "eruption" is a calculated attempt to contrast Trump and his opponent and to control the narrative with free media.

I don't believe in reactions. As a matter of disclosure, my early adult life was a series of reactions and eruptions which led me to anxiety, depression, and failure. I wholeheartedly believe in responses.

Responses are our calculation of what we believe, in terms of conviction, and what is appropriate for what has just happened. Sometimes these responses are seemingly immediate because the event is very familiar and we know how to prevail within it, and sometimes they are days or weeks in the making.

When Trump called the leader of North Korea, Kim Jong-Un, "Rocket Man" that was anything but a stream of consciousness comment or knee-jerk reaction to Kim Jong's nuclear efforts. This was likely a fleeting thought over several days or weeks that Trump had experienced as North

Korea tested nuclear weapons and failed. In his mind, it was passively derogatory. He likely percolated on the phrase for several days before saying it on the stage at the United Nations. He knew exactly how much attention such a comment would receive. He knew it wasn't a professional or 'presidential' comment. He predicted precisely how the media would react. He knew without a doubt that the elite losers of our political establishment in America would react with fear mongering that Trump was about to create an unnecessary nuclear war.

He also knew that discussing North Korea, as one of the most serious news stories of our time, was not a ratings generating story and thus was being ignored by the media. In order to make sure it garnered the attention, he had to manipulate….uh…hmmm… deliver the statement in a way that would create outrage.

As a result, he probably suspected that such a comment would create an intense discussion and train the world's attention on a hidden threat that many were ignoring. In other words, simply stating in a professional and presidential way that Kim Jong-Un and North Korea threatened the world with potentially inevitable nuclear war, would neither have created attention nor any real reaction.

Two very unpresidential words, 'Rocket Man', created a debate that paragraphs of professional and 'presidential' words never would or could.

I say again that every tweet, statement, and response is extremely calculated once you find the Trump in you, and that you should never apologize just because of the reaction your actions create in other people.

This book is not about selling you on conservative policy, Trump policy, or even the qualities of Trump as a person. This book is about the propensity to be consumed by others and distract from your own potential. If you are already respected by many, this book probably explains why. If you are a Trump hater, this is not about changing your opinion. This is about connecting you to the unique traits within you, just like Trump discovered and used, so that you can understand and achieve success.

Just remember, apologies destroy your purpose and conviction. The best way to respond to a demand for an apology that seemingly asks you to be in conflict with your values is to say "I regret my convictions have created this reaction in you."

 By the way, take note of friends, relatives, and colleagues that apologize frequently. They don't mean a damn word of it!

I once had some friends fire me as the listing agent of their home. The following day I cornered them on the phone and demanded to know why they were firing a friend and asking to unilaterally breach an active contract. I won't bore you with the litany of reasons except to say that they were financially desperate and made a series of decisions before I became involved that were now producing very negative financial consequences. As a result, they had a need for an immediate solution without the ability to sacrifice price to create it. In other words, they wanted more money than the home was worth in less time than the market was producing.

After a lengthy discussion, they apologized for firing me. I responded by saying "if you're sorry that you're firing me then that must mean that you wish to continue with me right?" Obviously I already knew the answer. The apology was an attempt to diminish my offended reaction. There must've been two dozen apologies in that phone call.

Toward the end of the call I expressed that I didn't believe they were sincere in any of their feelings about firing me. I suggested that they were desperate in that they were willing to stomp over anyone in order to recklessly prove to themselves that they could accomplish what was impossible. I told them bluntly that until they got their price in line the home was not going to sell. That fell on deaf ears. It usually does.

Since there was a friendship predating the listing agreement I felt the need to be a friend one last time. I told them that "your own worst enemy is you. You created this situation by spending too much on renovations. Until you recognize that you take no advice from anyone and you first seek to placate your emotions before making logical decisions, you will continue to have disruption and failure in life. I cannot be the victim of such fallout by a friend who consistently does this to themselves."

That moment was the 'Trump in me.' Since receiving the email 'firing my ass,' discussing it with a mutual friend, and enduring the ridiculous reasons for the firing, I had calculated a response based upon my value system. Here it is: always tell the truth to my friends. Make tough decisions about friends to remove toxicity in my life. Say things to people that they need to hear not for my benefit but for theirs. If you've been used and abused (as I was in this situation), get over it. Move on, quickly. And, finally, don't put up with bull shit!

This entire situation was "bull shit." It was ridiculous and offensive. I want to be successful in life while building deep, meaningful relationships. To do this, I have to allow people to tell me who they really are. This doesn't mean they're bad people. In fact, I learned that these attacks or abuses likely have nothing to do with me at all. I also know it's not my job to 'fix' anyone or to force anyone to change. It's only my role to stand up for myself, my rights, and what I believe to be right while being fair and truthful with others.

In most cases, everything I've just described, above, is explained by saying "Bryan only cares about money. He's a terrible friend. The friendship was insignificantly valued at the minimal level of a single real estate deal." In most people's eyes, my fleeting words of advice might as well have been "you have the ugliest child in the world, your mother is a whore, you're fat, and your face is ugly." Of course I would've never said that as a reaction to being fired on a real estate deal, but my constructive criticism was heard, nonetheless, just as destructively as that. That's how losers hear constructive advice and criticism.

 And that's how media and political losers hear everything Trump said too: in the worst possible contextual interpretation. I'm not saying they were always wrong. I'm saying they were mostly wrong.

 My reaction to this friend was not about being fired. It was about consistently having the experience of investing in a relationship the provided my family and me nothing in return. I couldn't continue helping a friend do what was in their best interest only to realize I was enabling them to continue being stupid by avoiding being candid. It was not about money here. It was about my mental health and leaving a friendship with the simple feeling "I have no regrets and I gave them advice that if taken will serve them well."

 In full disclosure, the next scenario I'm going to describe never really happened. But I've had hundreds of such similar scenarios. I want to spare you the verbosity of giving you another story about a failed friendship and simply share a similar anecdote. Also, even though I've named no one personally, in this book, everyone I've mentioned in any perceived negative tone will have a mental breakdown when/if they read it especially if they haven't changed.

Let's say that I was running for mayor of a small city in South Carolina. Again I never did, but humor me here. Let's say that one of my opponents was the friend I just described. We both entered the race and we presented our policies and vision for the city. Unexpectedly, my former friend started attacking me as a person only concerned about money. They claimed I was "self-consumed and narcissistic." I then responded by telling a story of how destructive and sloppy this person was in living their life. Do you see where I'm going with this?

Let me throw out a few names just in case you're not following me here: "Low-Energy Jeb" (Jeb Bush), "Crooked Hillary" (Hillary Clinton), and "Sloppy Steve" (former Trump advisor Steve Bannon). Do you get my drift?

These are all people that at one point called themselves friends of Donald Trump. At some point, except "Sloppy Steve," they begged him for campaign donations. They cozied up, rode Trump's coattails, and had absolutely no problem being associated with him until he shockingly became their political opponent. In the context of politics, and at the time the writing of this book, they also earned the moniker of "losers," mostly as a result of attacking Trump. As a result Trump destroyed them. He has always said "I'm a counterpuncher."

You and I both will let people into our lives that we will deeply regret. We're going to reveal weaknesses in ourselves that will come back to bite us. These perceived friends will use it against us. The only thing we can do is remove them from our inner circle as quickly as we figure out who they are and to defend ourselves vehemently and aggressively when they attempt to destroy us.

This may sound like a very cynical view of life. It's not. It's an observation of the formula behind success or failure. Assuming you're not living your life out of the pursuit of money or material things (which creates evil behavior), exposing frauds for who they are is part of everyone's calling.

Again, apologies are not needed for actions that support your convictions. Regret regarding other people's reactions is always appropriate. I simply regret what I cannot control. I regret that my friend made a decision to fire me because of a series of bad decisions they had already made.

 In the fictional scenario of my friend attacking me in order to defeat me, I regret having to destroy them in order to defend myself, but I'm damn sure not going to apologize for it. I will never reveal the intimate secrets I've learned of someone during the course of a legitimate friendship for the sake of my own advancement. You shouldn't either. But, if someone attempts to reveal intimate secrets about me in order to destroy my efforts, they have now unilaterally permitted me to expose what I had previously considered off-limits in order to defend myself. After all, they are attempting to take their 'feelings' resulting from a complex personal friendship completely out of context to fraudulently paint me as a 'bad person.'

 Read this how you want, but I refuse to apologize for the response I felt compelled to give because of the unprovoked, inappropriate, and personal attack of someone who thinks winning is more about destroying the opponent at all costs than maintaining their own personal convictions and abilities.

Many of the people who demand apologies out of people like me or President Trump do so because they are jealous that they've never developed the ability to live their life by not compromising their values and convictions.

I forgive them, almost instantly. It's not about me. It's not about you. And I realize that apathetic and listless people have no control over how threatening a convicted, passionate, and unapologetic person can be. Finding the 'Trump in You' can be lonely, leaving you with just a few friends.

I'd much rather have the four to five incredibly close friends I have, than dozens of relationships with fake, apathetic people who stand for everything but ultimately stand for nothing.

CHAPTER FIVE
The Secret to Success

 Without much effort, I finished high school near the top of my class. I was one of 3,000 students selected for the President's Emerging Leaders scholarship for college. I put no effort into any of it. I hated school, and I especially hated being tested by some bureaucratic geek's questions on a critical test that was designed to trick me into providing the wrong answer.

This chapter outlines the biggest difference between someone who reaches their potential and has a moderate level of success and someone who reaches their potential and becomes a billionaire. It has nothing to do with a test score, degree, the number of years you attend college, or how well you can recite the text of a book.

 This is not to dismiss the disciplines, analytical skills, and resolve that school teaches you. Let's face it. The biggest obstacle for me was that I hated school. It was one of my biggest successes to not only finish high school, but to do well in the process. By the time I got to college, I decided I would be better served getting real experience instead of being indoctrinated into compliance. My only regret about not finishing college was that it's one of the few things in my life I simply quit.

 The reality is that finishing college has very little to do with whether you will succeed in life unless you plan to be something like a doctor or lawyer. The real difference between most Americans and the roughly 600 billionaires of the world is just their career and family balance. Billionaire status may be appealing in theory but it requires a series of sacrifices that most people will choose to avoid.

 Coming up with a disruptive, revolutionary, and culture altering overnight success such as Mark Zuckerberg did with Facebook is a rare exception. Many of us measure our success or lack thereof against people like Zuckerberg whose overnight success was over a decade in the making with a lot of hard work and a good bit of luck.

 Some dismiss Zuckerberg as a guy who stole someone else's idea and as a fraud. If that makes you feel better about yourself, run with that. In reality, most billionaires are created by a concept they 'stole' from someone else, added significant value to and perfected. I call that "smart business."

Before Zuckerberg was 30, he was one of the richest people in the world. It's likely the first 30 years of his life have been extremely unbalanced, consumed by business, rocky relationships, and the loss of many friends and family relationships along the way. Zuckerberg has so much money that he can use it as a tool to find balance because he earned it not from years of hard work and risk but simply by being in the right place at the right time and creating something brilliant that the world desires.

He didn't imagine the success in terms of the amount of money Facebook would create for him. He simply had a passion for a service that revolutionized the way humans communicate. It's not to say that he doesn't deserve credit for the brilliance behind Facebook. He just didn't do it for the money. In fact, the money has probably been more a hindrance to his creativity than a help.

Sometimes we get consumed by watching the kind of success people like Zuckerberg experience and we lose sight of the fact that it wasn't created on purpose. There was a lot of hard work and ingenuity behind Facebook. No one can design and create that on purpose. It's a process of being inquisitive, timely, dedicated, and attempting to significantly change or disrupt something.

In fact you could put 100 times the work and sacrifice into your craft or purpose and never get even a fraction of the result that Zuckerberg has received.

You can be just as happy as Zuckerberg with a few hundred thousand dollars in retirement having lived your purpose and enjoyed important moments with a balanced life. You could have a better life than Zuckerberg with a fraction of the money because you have balance.

Life is not about money. People who pursue their interests for the sake of money never obtain it and keep it. They may obtain a lot of money, but it can disappear even faster.

About 20 years ago, I opened a real estate company. In my first year I made well over six figures. Within five or six years the company was producing seven figures per month and I mean dollars not house value volume. We had multiple offices in two states. We had franchised with a top national firm and became the number two franchise of hundreds in our brand system.

The anxieties and depression that I had faced in the late 1990s had become a distant memory. I was rarely anxious but very driven. I spent nearly every waking hour analyzing and calculating how to recruit more real estate agents, stay ahead of market trends, and build our revenue and market share.

It started to become work. We had gotten to this point because I was having so much fun watching my company grow and enjoying the exceptional relationships that my business family created. It was rewarding to watch people climb out of dead end jobs and become six figure income earners in the course of a year or two. It was most rewarding to watch them invest in housing, improve their family's situation, and save for retirement in a way they never could have done before.

Sometimes we get ahead of ourselves. We forget the secret sauce that got us to where we are. Sometimes with a false sense of humility it's easy to forget 'who built that.' There's always an "I" behind every successful company and team. I forgot that the secret sauce was me. Don't get me wrong. I had some awesome people around me and without them I couldn't have accomplished a fraction of what we did as a team.

What I just said may cause a number of people to stop reading this book instantly. They may see that statement as selfish and dismissive to the others who worked hard to help me succeed.

But, never forget that when you've had a dream and put it in motion and it's successful that it was you that created and unleashed that potential.

After a couple years of wild profits I bought a house on the water, then another one, then an expensive car, and expensive trips. Uh-oh!

In the midst of all of this I had found my soulmate and got married. 2006 was a great year, personally. It's also a year in which I have many business regrets. It was an experience I'll never forget because it was a fairytale year.

I had two waterfront homes, a second home on Sanibel Island in Florida on the beach, a cabin cruiser docked on the intra-coastal waterway near the Charleston Harbor minutes from the Atlantic Ocean. I had the car of my dreams, millions of dollars, and the chance to retire before I was thirty. I could have walked away then and never worked another day in my life.

I don't regret staying the course. What I regret is that now my dream and my passion had become distorted into a pursuit of money, extravagance, and material things. All this wonderful stuff was a big fat boat anchor, dragging me down, and consuming my time and resources.

This pursuit would cost me everything I learned, nearly cost me my marriage, and would fracture everything in my life.

When I said "God had a plan for me" in the first chapter, I wasn't kidding. He was about to give me an experience that no college can provide and that I could never have imagined.

I never struggled financially and I never had the thought of being in a marriage that could end. My parents have been married for four decades and my wife's the same.

During the throes of the worst financial crash since the Great Depression I was ignoring my wife and son and trying to save my ass. After 12 to 18 months of this nightmare, it suddenly occurred to me that the pursuit or possibility of any amount of money isn't worth the toxicity that these extravagances had brought to my life. Risk is unavoidable. However, failing to calculate that risk and your tolerance measured against the balance we all need in life is idiotic.

It's in these moments of imbalance that we find the purpose of our lives. My life was anything but balanced in 2008 and 2009 but it was about to change. All those years of wild success, unfettered income, and extravagant assets evaporated in mere moments. The balance for me was that I went from one extreme of success to another extreme of failure. And, all of my close friends and family got the displeasure of riding in my sinking ship with me.

There was no balance while I was fighting for my financial life. I was more absent from family and friends and not a pleasant person. The pursuit of money has a way of giving you extreme pendulum swings in life that are not worth experiencing. People will always find balance. It will either come through having incredible periods of wild success followed by extremely volatile and disruptive periods. You can also develop a consistent, moderated balance between family and business. This 'consistent moderation' presents a more boring, less stimulating experience. However, you will find more deep meaningful relationships with family and friends while having more predictable financial success as well. You won't necessarily become a billionaire on this plan, but you'll avoid the disruptions that many people find in the pursuit of just money.

Owning dozens of properties at that time and attempting to stop the financial hemorrhaging I was facing, required me to humble myself to embrace foreclosures and negotiate short sales or settlements with banks on nearly everything. I developed a skill very early that was about to be in huge demand.

By the time most Americans were facing foreclosure, significant household job loss, and the bottom of a pit of despair, I had collapsed financially, gotten back on my feet, and was making insane money again.

I remember it like this: It's like I woke up one day in 2011/2012 and said, "Holy Shit! I'm making more money now than I was before the collapse! How did that happen?" This may sound impossible to believe, but I literally had gone two years without thinking about money as a definition of success.

This time, I knew God had given me the skills that were in high demand to help people in that moment and I was called to do something with them.

 I helped thousands of people save their homes from foreclosures and short sales. My radio show was reinvented to help people understand how to battle what I would call "Evil Banks" and avoid "the frauds" - people preying on the vulnerable offering false hope and false promises of help to those facing complete financial devastation. I refused to profit off of someone's continued financial demise. I would only profit when and if I could repair or improve their situation. It was a newfound "golden rule" for me.

 I used my horrific, personal experiences to become a whistleblower and a consumer advocate. I personally worked with hundreds of radio show listeners who called me to save their house from foreclosure. We saved nearly all of them either through a short sale or by putting them with legitimate mortgage modification companies who could restructure their payments so they could keep their home.

 I developed a list of service providers that they could trust and when they took advantage of people I stepped back in to fix it and never used those providers again.

Here's where finding balance brings you more reward than you could ever imagine. It's hard to sit in a family's home staring at a quick $30,000 commission and actually migrate to making nothing from your efforts but helping them keep it. Simply by giving them the right advice could be the flash point between them being out on the street and keeping their home and family stable for many years to come.

Three years earlier, I would have simply convinced them to sell without regard for what was the best and most Christian thing to do. Even if you're not Christian, you can understand my values by reducing my religion to simply being loving. Love does not include harming people for your own gain.

What I quickly learned is that for every commission I lost for dispensing the best consumer advice, three or four more would appear. The people I helped to save their homes became huge advocates in finding me new business opportunities. I was getting referrals from people who I may have spent 30 to 60 minutes helping.

Building trust with people is more important than any amount of money a single relationship can provide. That is balance. You accept that some business is not right in exchange for more business than you ever thought possible that is.

Regardless of what you've seen in the media, you rarely find an ex-business partner of President Trump, regardless of their politics, that has anything convincingly negative to say about him. Certainly his competitors bash him. People on the other side of a business deal who couldn't figure out how to take advantage of him bash him. Political opponents build armies of people to attack by using false outrage. But, you rarely find the people in Trump's life that were closest to him who have anything but glowing testimony about their experiences.

Winning is about pursuing your dreams, silencing the clutter of numerous naysayers, and not stomping on the dreams of others. "Not stomping" includes "not harming" as well.

While most Americans are focused on what they don't have and what other people think of them, the most successful are pursuing their passions and dreams with unwavering conviction. If you become the latter, you will invite a lot of blowback, criticism, and disruptive attacks from people trying to slow you down.

These attacks are not about you. It's never about you when they do this. Watching someone I know or a close competitor do better than me used to eat me alive. I was never a jealous person but I defined my competitiveness by market share and dollars. There's nothing wrong with this, except when it's your primary focus.

Fortunately, this wasn't a huge crutch, because I didn't mind other people winning as long as I was on top. In fact, I love seeing other people win and don't mind sharing success. I'm not threatened by being number two so long as I've met my goals in the process.

Finding balance becomes defining winning in your own healthy and meaningful terms. We tend to define winning as getting a specific trophy, being in first place, or having the most money. That's allowing society to define our life and what success is.

What I described to you about my financial recovery and helping people is a secret formula to success and balance that very few people ever find. Loosely translated: focus on the activities that are required on a consistent and daily basis not on the outcome that you desire.

We will get to this in a later chapter, but it's important to note here: before you can make and keep a ton of money you must have found your purpose and created a vision for what you want your life to be 5, 10 even 20 or 30 years from now. Who do I want to be with? What do I want to be doing? What do I want to be able to afford and why? What do I want people to say about me looking back at my career or life? These questions are the tip of the iceberg and the answers do not come easily.

Once you define the answers, everything you do in life thereafter is measured against whether it's accomplishing that mission or not.

For me, that mission has always naturally been inside me since I was a teenager. It's why I did so well in school helping my high school colleagues with our newspaper, television, and radio department. My freshman English teacher was the leader of that department and invited me to join after spending time with me my freshman year. She saw talents in me that would have taken me years to discover.

I've made a point not to give specific names of people in this book that have had positive or negative influence in my life for various reasons. For this story, I feel compelled to make an exception because there is no greater reward for most teachers than knowing they have made a significant impact on a child that is positive and lasting for a lifetime.

Mrs. Judy Stanley, my freshman English teacher for the class of 1995 at Springfield High School in Springfield, Tennessee, gets full credit for being the first person responsible for putting me on a path that most people never discover. She saw something in me I would likely have never seen myself and is likely single-handedly responsible for my ability to write this book, talk on the radio, and close a real estate deal. She empowered me to unleash my potential at an early age.

Many people simply don't have this experience with another person or miss it when they do.

The next monumental moment was when I applied for the President's Emerging Leaders Scholarship in 1995 at Austin Peay State University and was 1 of 15 students out of 3,000 accepted. It was stunning because I had never thought of myself as a leader in the least even though that is exactly what I had been doing for the last three years of high school thanks to Mrs. Stanley.

Fast forward to today. All of this translates into a purpose of helping people find their potential, holding powerful and wicked people accountable, and translating my financial successes into helping the most vulnerable children of our society.

Notice I said many Americans never have a Mrs. Stanley. We all owe it to our society to become a Mrs. Stanley for other people and help them escape the hell of the inner city or abusive parents and simultaneously find their significant purpose. We are failing as a society in this regard.

If the business proposition, friend, or colleague stands to diminish that purpose, I'm out. My platform has to be much larger, my reach has to be significant and I am called to drive significant dollars and attention to the things that ail our culture the most. This means money transitions from being a way to buy endless stuff I don't need into making a difference in the world around me.

Now back to the activities. The activities that accomplished my goals during the financial crash and my financial recovery had zero focus on money. I clearly knew how much money I needed to keep moving forward and to meet my realistic lifestyle expectations. However, I never focused on the money.

 I set out to help as many people as possible. This meant sometimes I would get a huge commission check for helping people. At other times, I'd get paid nothing.

 Life is about balance. If I approach this dilemma and destructive time simply by helping people and I'm simultaneously exceeding my financial goals why focus on the money? I had been teaching my agents this principle as individuals and had failed to apply it to my own life, until then.

 When you define the outcome and then let it go it's only then that you'll meet or exceed it.

 I love sports analogies for these principles and disciplines. In my opinion, the Alabama Crimson Tide football program under the leadership of Head Coach Nick Saban is the best sports legacy we've ever seen. It's produced nearly two dozen popular head coaches, dozens of superstar NFL players, and multiple national championships.

 I have such respect for Nick Saban as a business person, a coach, and an individual that I cannot overstate it. I can guarantee you that Saban never thought about the money, yet he's earning more than virtually every other NCAA football coach in America and setting records for contractual income.

The secret sauce to winning in sales, life, or sports is to reduce the most complex things to the simplest tasks. This reminds me of the phrase, "how do you eat an elephant?" The answer is "one bite at a time!"

 A simple explanation of Saban's formula is this: keep your eyes off the scoreboard. While I'm sure he never says it this way, let me explain. Keep your eye off the scoreboard (distraction), means "don't worry about winning the football game and go out there on this down and give me one yard more than you gave me last time."

 My son loves basketball, but as I watch him play, he frequently looks at the score. My best advice to him is to stop worrying about the score or the clock and focus only on how to get that round ball through the net as quick as possible. I also tell him, as a backup, that if you don't see an opportunity in a split second look for a teammate who has one, throw him the ball, and tell him to shoot it. This is loosely called leadership: Take the shot if you can. If you can't, help someone else on your team do it.

Since he's a point guard, that gives him a chance to be an exceptional leader. His back-up plan is looking for opportunities other people have that they don't even know exist.

If he's distracted by the clock or the scoreboard, the clock is going to run out and they're going to lose the game by not making the shot. He'll probably miss the chance to give his teammate an opportunity that neither will see.

Just to keep us on track, we'll tie all of this back to Trump soon. Stay with me.

I learned this lesson in CrossFit, not business. That's probably why the research shows that people who continue a discipline of fitness and maintain a healthy body mass earn 12% more money in their career.

In CrossFit, there are guys who can bench press three or four hundred pounds, and do barbell squats of nearly the same. These guys are disciplined and their fitness objectives include a much different purpose than mine.

CrossFit programs normally end with what's called a WOD. It's usually three or four timed fitness activities. It could look something like this: power clean 135 pounds 10 times, run 6 laps, then do 20 pull-ups. I'm screwed!

All of my strength is in my lower body. At times I couldn't even do one round of the WOD let alone three. Fighting for my success and balance in CrossFit required me to modify my goals. I could run circles around the strong guys while they could barely run at all. That was my strength and I defined it. At times I would do more than demanded of me. But, I would use bands to help me reach the pull up number and lower the weight on the power cleans. Was this cheating?

No! It was finding balance and not turning this in to a competition. I was only competing with myself. The only competition every time I did WOD was to the beat Bryan Crabtree from the last time he did it. I had no interest in going to CrossFit competitions.

Over time, I was able to actually beat the much stronger guys as I struggled through the full 135-

pound cleans, mostly unassisted pull-ups, and running twice as fast as they did. If I had been focused on them instead of me I would have never gotten past the power cleans the first time. Instead, I could sometimes achieve a top time, simply by modifying my approach and utilizing my advantages and strengths.

While seizing on my strengths, I found that my weaknesses naturally diminished and eventually improved anyway.

Stop focusing on the competition. Identify your strengths and make modifications to isolate your weaknesses. Then produce something more than you did last time, every time.

I spent a lot of time in this chapter talking about balance and its role in success. Finding the 'Trump in You' is about finding these imbalances in your career. Without a doubt, the 45th president has mastered it.

But, the President also has failures resulting from his lack of focus on personal imbalance. Being extremely rich always invites a lot of people who care nothing about you except for your money. You'll probably never see them again if you were to lose your fortune, so who needs these people around?

Spending nearly every waking hour focused on being the best business person and doing the most successful business deals creates terrible personal and family imbalance. Most billionaires, or those close to it, suffer from divorce, lost friendships, and loneliness at an alarming rate.

They sold their personal balance in exchange for a business legacy that will be studied for decades after their death.

So, while this book explains how to find the 'Trump in You' and the secrets behind his success, it in no way suggests that you miss your children's childhood and ignore your friends or your spouse in the process of doing it. There's more to life than 'The Art of the Deal' even though I highly suggest you read that book.

Sometimes being a footnote in the history books produces a more balanced and successful life than being a chapter in it.

You have to make that choice when you define how you want your life to look. And if you define family as a major part of that objective you will have to be willing to pass on opportunities, and the potential profits, in order to achieve what you want.

CHAPTER SIX
Manifesting the Impossible

Many writers have compared Apple founder Steve Jobs and Donald Trump. The similarity lies in the fact that both of them have a history of stating impossible, nearly unbelievable goals, which magically seem to transpire on a predictable basis.

The title of this chapter might be better called "dreamers." The secret to both Jobs' and Trump's wild success is that they have broken through the mental barriers that society places on most people. Most average Americans, including the mainstream media, react to the bold statements of these types of individuals with a dismissive attitude. In many cases they call their statements lies, not recognizing that they are dreams.

Everyone has nagging dreams and desires inside of them, but most people are cultured not to listen to them. We have voices in our head that say, "don't do that - it's not responsible," or "it's not possible." This is a condition most Americans developed from a sense of fear implanted by an increasingly defeatist society.

Imagine for a moment being a person who doesn't fear failure. Imagine not worrying about what someone thinks about you if you do fail. If you can empathize with those emotions you can understand why Donald Trump is such a polarizing figure to so many people.

Not everyone will live their dreams, but everyone can. This is a core belief of successful change agents like Jobs and Trump.

At this point, I should interject the phrase "fake it until you make it." There are many writings about Trump that connect the quandary of how he can be so successful without succeeding. On the journey to success you have to first create the perception of success. This perception is invaluable in attracting the right people, closing the right deals, and sourcing the capital to get your dream off the ground.
Most people believe you have to 'pay your dues' and 'wait in line' on your journey to the top. This is a recipe for failure. The idea of 'paying your dues' comes from a society of people who want competition to stay in line behind them while they exert little to no effort to compete. Most successful people have solved a problem for which the masses have only complained about. Paying your dues is a complete waste of time.

The key ingredient to Jobs' and Trump's success is disruption. In the beginning Jobs disrupted the computer industry by creating a desktop version of what had been historically a bedroom sized mainframe. In other words, he took the ideas of an established company like Xerox or IBM for business and delivered them into the homes of millions of Americans.

Jobs was judged based upon his outward appearance and not his ability to deliver to the market something everyone needed but no one wanted. Over time, he revolutionized computing, the music industry, how we consume content/audio, and created an entire market of smart phones that combined all of his intentions into one with the iPhone. He didn't invent any of these devices or genres. He simply disrupted existing industries by giving consumers a better version of what already existed.

Along the journey, Jobs was fired from the company he invented, decried as a tyrant, and disgraced in every industry he touched. These rebukes were because he was a significant threat and his vision was so far ahead of his competitors that no one could imagine what was coming next. He was so brilliant it was very difficult to understand what the hell he was talking about most of the time.

This frustrated Jobs so much that he was frequently called an "asshole" because of his desperate attempts to force people to understand his vision.

The shocking aspect of Jobs' journey is that his dreams were a joke to nearly everyone but him. This dismissal gave him an unfettered platform to turn them into reality.

Trump is no different.

The reality of Trump's political aspirations and ascent to the presidency was no differently received than any activity that made him a multibillionaire. As a presidential candidate he was dismissed as nothing more than a joke. But he won!

In the late 1970s, Trump entered the cutthroat world of Manhattan real estate. He didn't just enter Manhattan real estate, he decided to build a luxury brand of high-end hotels and condominiums. His first big move was met with the same dismissal as his presidential aspirations.

Much like Jobs, he found a market that didn't exist before his entry. He would find troubled or dilapidated properties in transitional areas and build luxury brands. Who builds a five star hotel in 'the hood?' Trump does.

Knowing that he was about to reshape an entire city block, he could take real estate positions in anticipation of future value. After all, he was doing legal insider trading and he was the market maker. These landholding positions would disrupt the orderly flow of business as usual in Manhattan real estate because people would find out not only had he transformed the city block, he had also been so confident in his success, he bought 'chunks' of the block so he didn't raise the values for anyone but himself.

Is this selfish? Who cares! It's damn smart.

Much like Apple, the Trump brand in real estate was known for exceptionalism. It would command a higher price which resulted in much larger profit margins. No one liked this because they missed the fact that Trump and Jobs were master branders. They could convince you that you desperately needed to buy something you didn't want and didn't really need by making it so appealing and chic it was unavoidable.

The loser mentality that frequently prevails in our society has a propensity to focus on Jobs' firing from the company he created, Apple's near bankruptcy, or the fact that the company that invented the personal computer Apple lost market share to Microsoft. This viewpoint dismisses the reality that Apple was about creating disruptive experiences and not necessarily about owning the market. Without a doubt, Jobs and Apple disrupted our culture more than any company in the last hundred years. They changed the way we hear music, see video, communicate, and collaborate. As a result, they have over 90% of the profits in the smartphone market and almost every American now owns an Apple product.

Trump created a brand that equated to luxury. Over time, Trump would be defined by ventures that failed like casino bankruptcies or his personal failures of divorce. Again, losers will focus on the failures in order to dismiss the exceptionalism.

Trump also disrupted the real estate market by establishing a new genre of experience. He created a model based upon early successes in real estate development that allowed him to shift all of the risk to developers while maintaining the extra margin of profit created by the brand. He eventually removed the risk of owning the developments and simply sunk his teeth into a substantial chunk of the profit from it. While his presidency may alter the value of his creation, he created a model that many major real estate developers now use.

One of the greatest arguments in his business is how to substantiate the value of the Trump brand. In the process of creating this brand he also had to be deeply rooted in pop culture. He branded himself as a celebrity representing the potential of America at the highest levels. His name became associated with billionaire status, private jets, and extravagance. Most Americans yearn for a taste of the lifestyle synonymous with "Trump." A lot of people visit his hotels because they feel like for a fleeting moment they are living Trump's luxurious lifestyle.

Most people on television and in political circles of Trump hatred have never visited one of his properties and therefore have no idea what sort of exceptional experiences the Trump Company creates for its guests. Fortunately, I had and knew that this is a man who could definitely handle the White House. The customer service at a Trump Hotel is beyond exceptional. He is the visionary who created that.

In essence, instead of projecting humility, he projected the exact opposite, appealing to a clientele of people who are magnetized toward success. This is one of the reasons there is so much outrage against them in politics.

Trump forces you to focus on success or be intimidated by it. Those who are intimidated or offended by Trump feel this way because they believe it's wrong to project strength or applaud exceptionalism and extravagance. It is this extravagance and defiance of the norms that made him so wildly successful.

Most dreams worth achieving seem nearly impossible in the beginning. The naysayers in your life don't believe in themselves and have it even more difficult time observing other people who do.

The most successful people reject this negativity and channel their energy into proving others wrong. This leaves a wake of jealous, entitled, and shameful people ready to attack at every step along the way.

The political naysayers along Trump's path to the Presidency were systematically destroyed because they turned their own aspirations and energy toward defeating Trump instead of presenting their vision and the best version of themselves.

When you find the 'Trump in You' you will reject the negativity as 'loser mentality,' pursue your dreams even harder, and dig even deeper to find the opportunity that no one else can see because they are so focused on stopping you.

CHAPTER SEVEN
Being Liked Sucks!

In chapter four, I talked about the difference in being liked and being respected. The difference between a billionaire and a middle-class American trapped in a dead end job can be linked directly to this.

The people that are liked by the most by coworkers or their community typically achieve the least. These people seek approval in everything they do. They allow the people around them to control their dreams, aspirations, and style.

The truth is that if you are living out your potential, you're making others quite jealous. Once you are climbing the economic ladder, realizing the American dream, saving for retirement, and driving a nice car you've already outpaced most Americans. Even then, there are plenty of people who envy you and need to feel better about themselves by diminishing you. They don't believe in their ability to grow, so they want more successful people to become less successful.

We've all heard the stories of multimillionaires that drive an old beat-up pickup, eat at the local buffet, and never portray an image of wealth. But what have they done to serve their purpose or leave a legacy of value to future generations? What good is all of that money unless you teach people a lesson about success, purpose, and returning value? Maybe some do, but choose not to participate in the fanfare of doing so.

This book is not about wealth and getting rich. This book is about achieving a level of success that exceeds what society has set for you. This success doesn't happen by pursuing money or material things but by pursuing a dream, purpose, or passion that is deep within you.

What is deep within you is completely misunderstood by the people around you. Colleagues, friends, even family are much more comfortable if they feel they have some control over your direction. The idea of 'one of us' far outpacing 'the rest of us' is terribly uncomfortable. Probably, this means as you journey up the economic ladder, people will stop liking you if for no other reason than they are no longer holding you down to their level.

Most likable people aren't candid, avoid conflict, run the other way, and refuse to stare adversity in the face and deal with it when it strikes. This means they never grow from their strife or conflict. They live a life of ignoring the lessons we can learn from failure.

They're too selfish to tell people what they really think in an attempt to avoid the reaction it might create. They allow problems to fester from modest levels to the point where they become existential threats to their future success. Everyone loves a loser because losers are not threatening to anyone - except to the most successful people.

The 'person' I dislike most is someone too selfish to tell someone else something constructively critical even harsh that can really help them because they are more interested in being liked than being respected.

By contrast, candid people who readily deal with conflict generally cause great strife in those living with an apathetic or loser mentality. Put bluntly, people like Trump aren't likable. He never will be. I learned from my early depression that I wasn't that likable either and all the effort in the world wasn't going to change that. However, over your life's journey, people that were subject to your conflict resolution skills and candid feedback rise out of the ashes of mediocrity to become allies with a deep respect for your influence. Now, that's worth something!

This reality is one of the reasons very few former Trump employees came forward during his presidential election to speak ill of their experiences with him as an employer. Now, I realize many people reading this book will immediately turn to Google to find stories that prove this statement untrue. If that was your first reaction, you are living with a loser mentality. You can't get past your hatred for Trump long enough to take my point in the spirit of helping you.

Please work on that.

Over the years, Trump companies have employed over 100,000 people. Finding even a few hundred naysayers is expected. They likely were the apathetic people that refused any constructive or candid feedback and he fired their asses.

The reality is that most people that have had direct experience with Trump not only respect him, they like him. But, I can assure you that most people who started their relationship with him on the other side of the negotiation table didn't like him at all in the beginning.

Being liked is easy. Most government bureaucrats are likable especially within their own ranks. They follow arbitrary rules and standards, check little boxes with nearly zero accountability as to the quality of their completed tasks, and don't engage in conflict. As an example, in the government world, job hierarchy is more about time and tenure and less about quality and achievement. This is the quintessential 'pay your dues' world.

It disgusts me.

This also explains why so many government employees at various levels are so anti Trump. Trump is everything they are not. They do not like him and they never will. This is why I say "being liked sucks" because in this government run world you have to be one of them in order to be liked.

I've said this on my radio show dozens of times: "There is nothing inherently wrong with working for the government, but to do so requires you to sell your soul to them in the process."

Being respected by a few is better than being like by many. Once you have earned the respect of another human being, you have likely earned their trust as well. This explains why Trump made the statement that he could shoot someone on Fifth Avenue and probably not lose any support. While he said it in jest, he realizes that his supporter base is full of people who respect him and trust that he will do in the end what he promised.

By contrast, President Obama came into office with the support of millions of Americans who liked him. In the end, he earned very little respect. President George W. Bush met the same fate. Both followed the government protocol of the presidency. They succumbed to what many call "being presidential."

What "being presidential" really means is being willing to allow the people around you to poll test everything you say and so that you won't create any major political distractions. This is compliance not leadership. While you may maintain a higher approval rating throughout your presidency, you will become a footnote in American history.

The most respected presidents also share the legacy of being the most effective. Presidents that made major reforms, took us through difficult periods, and delivered us into booming economic cycles are respected. These presidents are Andrew Jackson, Abraham Lincoln, Theodore Roosevelt,

Franklin Roosevelt, John F. Kennedy, and Ronald Reagan. This is an apolitical list in terms of party affiliation. They are exceptional presidents in terms of the legacy they left for America.

These presidents didn't follow the path or style of the presidents before them. They redefined what 'being presidential' is for generations to come. They changed the direction of American history and they overcame the darkest periods of our country while setting a path of new economic prosperity yet to be imagined. Without them, this country would not be the leader of the free world.

There is something else all of these exceptional presidents have in common. Two of them were assassinated and all of them had assassination attempts on their lives. I think it's safe to say that there were a lot of people who didn't like them.

However, in terms of their positive effect they are among the most respected names in American history. Even if you don't respect one or more of them, take my point for your personal gain instead of focusing on your feelings about the person I've described.

By finding the "Trump in You" you will be able to find a way to stare adversity in the face, engage in constructive conflict, and be candid with those around you without worrying about the blowback you are likely to create. With much greater respect from those around you, you can develop an army of ambassadors that will help you reach your goals and achieve your dreams.

Remember, the people that like you are not likely to help you. Those that respect you will endorse you and 'charge the hill' with you in many of the battles of life.

Without this respect and your personal army, you will fail.

CHAPTER EIGHT
The Art of the Counterpunch

The quickest path to failure is to focus on taking down your competition in order to reach your goals and become successful. However, this does not give you a pass to ignore your competition like most people do.

I've often heard people say that focusing on your competition is wrong. What they actually mean is that being consumed by your competition distracts you from finding opportunities to win. In reality, you always have to know with who or what you are competing. This does not contradict my earlier statement to take your eyes off the scoreboard. It's perfectly acceptable to be aware of competition. It's completely wrong to be consumed by it.

One of the things candidate Trump said was that he is a "counterpuncher." But, what does that mean? That means he studies the competition and even gets friendly with some of them so that he can understand them better.

I've always believed in keeping your friends close and your enemies closer. Accordingly, one of my core values is to never use the intimate details you learn from within a relationship or friendship for my own selfish purposes. This means that I never seek to use the knowledge gained from a relationship or friendship against that person or their interests. In politics, we see this all the time.

Many of the people that now despise Trump politically have at one point or another had a close personal relationship with them or solicited donations for their campaigns from him. In many cases they were friends or allies. Once Trump entered the political fray, many of those individuals started to use their prior associations with Trump in order to attack him.

In doing so, they invited a counterpunch. I'm confused as to why they were so shocked he then felt invited to destroy them. Well, I'm not really confused. I'm just being kind instead of calling them "stupid."

That counterpunch usually was far more brutal than the original attack. There is nothing more important in life than relationships. When we abuse a relationship and the intimacy and confidentiality that is expected we invite all-out war that is ultimately damaging to both sides.

As we watched politician after politician with prior and intimate relationships with Trump launch their attacks, seemingly without provocation, it was obvious what would happen next. Trump had to play the nasty game of counterpunching with information he would've never used otherwise. He knew their weaknesses, branded them with it, and destroyed them.

After all, when you attempt to bring down a successful person who believes in winning by promoting his value proposition and you launch personal and petulant attacks on them, their defense of their positions and reputation usually includes damaging your credibility which inherently destroys your cause.

The best 'counterpunchers' are people who define their competitors, focus on the value of the solutions they offer, and only respond to personal attacks.

From the beginning of the Trump campaign, he was attacked by people who had been confidants and allies of his in the media. From the first speech announcing his candidacy where he called some immigrants 'rapists and murderers' the attacks started coming. Long-standing relationships Trump had with media celebrities were seemingly destroyed by that one campaign announcement speech.

The reality is that these people were just opportunists who wanted to attack for the sake of getting attention and certainly without regard to it being at Trumps expense. Most people take the Michelle Obama approach: "when they go low, we go high." The reality is that that never works.

We are built with a vast array of human instincts that are meant to protect us. Human instinct tells us to fight back when we are attacked physically or verbally. Very few people stand still while they're being assaulted physically. Almost everyone, regardless of their physical capacity, tries to fight off such an attack. Then, why do we take a different approach when we are verbally or socially attacked?

Why do you think venomous snakes strike when they feel threatened? Survival. That is inside all of us. Many of us allow others to destroy our reputations by preying on the petty reality that 'we want to be liked.'

Aside from our physical well-being, our mental and perceptual well-being are the most important assets we have. The loser mentality that has been perpetuated in our society tells the masses it is wrong to indulge someone's petulant attack with a similar response. By contrast, the reality is that no response typically is the biggest endorsement of any personal attack against you.

Okay. I know they say that being defensive makes you sound guilty. That's 'horse shit' peddled by people who want you to stand down and let them attack you.

Trump understands these principles and that's why he fights back with a strong counterpunch against anyone who is able to successfully mount a public attack on him.

Many focus on whether Trump is telling the truth or lying in his counterpunching. The reality is that the ferociousness of his attacks is more important than the veracity of them.

The art of the counterpunch is about creating consequences for people who decide to come after you with personal attacks. Most people can't handle the ferocious nature of Trump's counterpunch. Therefore, Trump creates a significant consequence to the reputations of those who attack him. You may disagree with this style, but it's very effective. People who may serve as the most credible witnesses to Trump's weaknesses (having worked closely with him) know the consequences for attacking and thus stay silent. This leaves less credible pundits and media analysts attempting to damage Trump and not those with the most intimate knowledge.

Are you more likely to intimidate a copperhead snake or a garden snake? Clearly, any sane person would intimidate neither for the sake of getting bitten. But you're more likely to die from a venomous copperhead bite than a non-venomous garden snake. No one is intimidating a copperhead unless they have access to anti-venom.

What these attacks result in are political attacks done mainly for the purpose of self-aggrandizement and voyeurism. In other words, the attacks never matter to the people whose hearts and minds the attacker wishes to change. They simply create meaningless confirmation of greatness from a crowded feedback loop of people in the same 'Hate-Trump' echo chamber.

The more these media and political Trump haters launch meaningless attacks against him, the more focus and power they give him to control the narrative on the issue that was the catalyst for the attack. Every time they attacked Trump and judged him as a person, without judging the issue, they validated his message.

Trump understands that if his messages keep being validated and he keeps being personally assailed, that eventually respect for his positions will turn into an unwavering respect for him as well. Most people never get close to this understanding in their lives.

Most Americans who are verbally attacked by someone are simply too emotionally weak to defend their reputation. Therefore most people internalize the kind of attacks that Trump has endured. They reject candid feedback. They avoid painful realities and over time they become addicted to feeling good.

If you can't fight for your own reputation, how can you fight for anything else in life? Why would someone like me want to help you and become involved if you can't even stand up for yourself? The more you take the abuse, the more you become what the abuser wants you to be. Over time you seek only validation and approval while avoiding some of the most important and critical feedback the world has to offer. It's this reason why many Americans are stuck in jobs they hate, not realizing their true potential and are angry at the world around them.

 I used to be amazed at real estate agents who would attempt to compete with me by reducing their fee from 6% to 4% or 5%. That's all they had? I would nail that loser approach every time by simply saying, "If they can't even fight for their own commission like I am, why in the world would you believe they will fight for your equity? That's insane!" 9 times out of 10, they were cooked.

 These negative people suck the life and prosperity out of the people they encounter. They explain most successes as cheating. They define others through their failures and not their accomplishments. They stop growing as people and professionals. They become victims with a deflated sense of self-worth and an inability to enjoy their accomplishments.

 These negative people are precisely why Trump won the election. While we may be offended by the things Trump says, we're even more offended by negative losers who attempt to win at the expense of others. We have a hard time articulating this, but many Americans voted for Trump not because they like him, but because they respect his accomplishments and disrespect the attempt to tell them how to vote by his opponents.

While the counterpunch may be what gets all of the negative attention, it's not what creates the toxicity. There are many successful people around all of us. There are just as many losers who believe the best way to win is by taking others down first

The 'Art of the Counterpunch' makes certain that doesn't ever happen.

Are you going to live your life by enduring and internalizing the attacks by the losers around you? Or, are you going to find winners who will give you critical feedback in an attempt to help you and not harm you? Are you going to keep letting society tell you when and where it's okay for you to stand up for yourself and what you believe in?

If you continue down such a path you may die with people around you that love you. But, will you have lived out your potential on earth or simply allowed others to steal it from you? God did not put us here to put a question mark at the end of our lives asking if we had done all our potential allowed. We are here to put an exclamation point at the end of our lives or at the very least a period.

Stop allowing people to abuse you. Draw boundaries with those who violate yours. Push back with the truth no matter how harsh it is and defend yourself at every turn because no one else will.

'The Art of the Counterpunch' is a necessity for winning in life and Trump proved my point by winning an election that no one could have predicted he would win. Well seemingly no one except people like me....

CHAPTER NINE
Disruption

Disruption may sound like a very negative term. It isn't.

At the center of every major success story, company, product, or service is severe disruption. The key ingredient to achieving all of your potential in your professional life, is to disrupt your industry or marketplace in a notable way.

In chapter six, I talked about how Steve Jobs disrupted the cell phone market, music industry, and personal computing market by successfully launching the first real mainstream smartphone: the iPhone. In reality, Jobs didn't invent the smartphone.

It may surprise you that IBM invented the smartphone in the 1990s with a product called the "Simon." It had very little success. No one wanted a smartphone. No one even understood why such a product was needed. Enter Steve Jobs. IBM wasn't very good at explaining to people why they needed their gadgets. They were so bad at it, that they are mostly now just a consulting firm.

What people wanted was a way to make their music more portable, easier to control, and downloadable. They wanted a more efficient way to check their email. By the time the iPhone was invented, cell phones were a primary form of telecommunications. Before the iPhone and iTunes, we were happy carrying around a pager, iPod, and flip phone.

In 2006 Steve Jobs figured out, not how to make a smartphone or even a portable computer but how to disrupt three industries at the same time. After that, he disrupted the software industry. Before the iPhone, we purchased the software on CDs to install on our computer. Now, 12 years later we purchase apps - billions of them each year.

The process of disruption is delivering a product or service that solves a major problem or tackles a problem that has yet to be identified.

In the real estate business in Manhattan, Trump disrupted the luxury condo and office market. You can refer back to chapter six for the details. What he did was deliver mixed-use luxury living before 'mixed-use' was a common term. He created something new in an industry of old.

Most Americans will never reinvent communication, change the music industry, or disrupt the automobile industry in a revolutionary way. However, we can always find ways to meaningfully disrupt our niche within industries.

I recently visited the White House for a "radio row" for the privilege of interviewing many of the top officials in the White House. Trump is already disrupting the way business is conducted at the White House. Almost every president gets up early, goes into a series of 'meetings about meetings,' and has worked half a day by nine or ten in the morning. Most White House meetings with the president don't start until after nine and sometimes as late as eleven.

I receive the schedule for the White House Press Corps every day and I still laugh as I see a nearly blank schedule until about noon each day.

What Trump is creating is a disruption to age old traditions that allowed no flexibility for creativity or free time for relaxation. If your day starts at 5 AM and ends at midnight, eventually your work quality will significantly erode.

This is a very minor form of disruption that can significantly and positively alter the conditions and productivity in the White House.

Why in the hell should people get up at 3 AM just to get to the White House to meet with the president at 6 AM? Why not just work a normal schedule that is more conducive to a normal life?

Apparently, the answer to this is "because it's the White House." Okay! That's a terrible answer. Trump said, "Change it. You'll now give me my intelligence briefing at 11 AM instead of 6 AM. Problem solved!" Everyone went nuts and then he reminded them that he was the president.

In your own business or workplace, you can find areas where productivity is hampered by dated and redundant processes. You can identify waste in the workplace.

I have a good friend who anchors news in one of America's largest cities. In essence, he was just a radio news anchor, and he still is. Looking around the newsroom, there were countless people doing brainless jobs that most industries had already replaced with computer automation. In addition, the quality all the broadcasts were hampered by the higher potential for human error. So, he created an automated system that allows anchors to control almost the entire broadcast without distracting them from the delivery of the news.

Most people react to this with loser mentality about all of the jobs he cost which were dead end jobs anyway. In reality, he created jobs writing code for his software and installing it on computers.

Over time, his software revolutionized this decades-old radio station and led to significantly higher productivity. Since he owns the software, do you think he has job security? Not only did he save his company potentially hundreds of thousands of dollars per year, he created additional income and job security in the process. He now sells this product to thousands of radio stations across the country. He didn't invent broadcast automation. He invented a product that fills a demand left void by the existing automation software.

Always be looking for an opportunity to solve a problem in your workplace or industry. Always pay attention to the needs in your personal life and see if anyone has invented a solution. If they have, and you can afford it, buy it. Your time and productivity are the only valuable commodities you have. If it's not available, then you may (and notice I say "may") have found a way to disrupt a niche or industry.

I told a friend who has a startup furniture company to go find someone who has tried everything in your industry to get it right, finally got it, and ran out of money. Take their idea, improve upon it, and own it. Is this stealing? Maybe. But it's also ingenious. Steve Jobs didn't invent the smartphone. He took someone else's failed attempt and made it actually work.

The most disruptive people are frequently called troublemakers. During the civil rights movement, Martin Luther King Jr. was frequently called a 'troublemaker' by the opposition. To them, he was. He was forcing society to face the fact that all people should be treated equally. Those that were winning because of inequality faced the proposition that they would lose influence and power if millions of African-Americans suddenly gained more of it.

We've already established that people who think this way are losers. They need others to lose for them to win.

In reality, Martin Luther King Jr. was a disruptor; certainly not a troublemaker. We see this because society embraced his vision for America and moved through a period of civil rights laws and measures that would begin to empower all Americans, not just some. In reality, the losers of the civil rights movement were 'the losers' of our society.

 The only people that lose in disruptions are people who refuse to embrace cultural, social, or professional revolutions. In our modern age, many people reject social media. The fact is that social media has disrupted the way we communicate. Those who oppose social media and refuse to embrace it will eventually find themselves unable to sell their products or services because they will become irrelevant.

 Many 'brick-and-mortar' businesses blame Amazon for 'killing retail.' The fact is, as of this writing, Walmart alone is still as large as the entire online retail economy. In five years, this will no longer be the case. But, how did bellwether brands like Circuit City, Toys "R" Us, Blockbuster Videos, and Tower Records end up in bankruptcy?

 They didn't recognize the writing on the wall. Walmart did. In 2021, the online retail business will be twice the size of Walmart Today, it's virtual parity. Walmart recently announced the closure of 60 Sam's Club stores for the main purpose of turning them into distribution warehouses. They purchased Jet.com. They are perhaps the only remaining company with the strength and fortitude to make a major shift in their business model without destroying their livelihood.

Walmart recognized that consumers are never going to flock to Walmart.com like they do Amazon.com. There's just something about a 'brick-and-mortar' business that keeps us from naturally buying online with the same intensity. Part of the problem is that an online business must have significantly different delivery times, return policies, and checkout procedures. Consumers still want their products quickly and brick-and-mortar is synonymous with 'slow.'

 What Walmart has done is almost unprecedented. They closed stores creating a shockwave in the retail business. The stores were closed not because they weren't making money. They were closed because they could performance better as distribution centers to increase delivery time for its online operation.

Walmart also understood that purchasing an online brand like Jet.com, would immediately eliminate the perception of being a slow 'brick-and-mortar' retailer. While there's never a way to truly predict how these measures succeed or fail, over time, I'm rather confident I'll be writing a book in the next decade about how Walmart backstopped Amazon. And, if it's not Walmart, it will be someone else because of similar reasons.

Whether it's a business as large as Walmart or middle class workers, we will be significantly impacted by disruption in our lives and industries many times in our lives. The best way to benefit from disruption is to create more of it by evolving ahead of others or by solving a problem no one else has or will.

Trump disrupted politics. For decades, Americans have complained that politicians were detached and even liars. Most politicians were victorious in runs for political office by using focus groups and political experts to manufacture a message that will connect to the most people even if it was totally disingenuous. With everyone seemingly playing a disingenuous game of 'Hollywood acting' to win public office, our political process was ripe for extreme disruption.

Trump listened to callers on talk radio stations across America for the year prior to his campaign launch. He heard them cry, scream, and worry. His messages were crafted to fix the problems of everyday Americans. Many conservatives worried that these too were disingenuous messages. His record clearly shows the opposite.

Trump disrupted politics by saying the exact opposite of what political experts have long told the political class to say. He attacked the Gold Star dad who used his son's death as a shield for his self-enriching immigration law firm. Political experts have long told politicians not to challenge the families of the fallen, even if their message is illicit. Trump pointed out that Arizona Senator John McCain was a war hero, but that he preferred heroes who were captured. In historical terms, such a comment should have been the end of his career. But, the opposite occurred because he pointed out in a simple statement that John McCain had long used a decades-old event to shield himself from being held as fully accountable as some of his colleagues. The list of such 'political career-ending statements' by Trump is too long to list here.

Each of them had a theme for Trump: say what I think and mean what I say. Trump seized on something I've long known to be true.

Consistently telling people what you believe, why you believe it, and what it means (no matter how controversial or outside of mainstream) is far more valuable to your success than becoming a disingenuous parrot. People in this country yearn for authenticity, individuality, and sincerity. They yearn for it so much, in such a fake world, that they are willing to overlook even the worst aspects of a guy like Trump.

Oddly, Trump disrupted our political process and especially the Republican Party by simply speaking his mind and refusing to apologize for it.

Disruption is created out of a genuine desire to make a difference, create change, and solve problems. The reactions of the establishment political class to Trump are really a reaction to themselves. They are resentful that they have become powerless experts and that Trump gets to win by simply being himself.

Whether you like Trump's rhetoric, phraseology, and style or not you must recognize the power in simply being real. In a world consumed by indignation and 'fakeness,' being real is disruptive and transformative.

There is a disruptor in everyone including you. Find 'The Trump in You' by making a difference and creating a disruption that can move you closer toward your goals and purpose. Don't let society tell you that your convictions are wrong. Show society where they are right.

People love to follow those who have strong opinions and stand by them whether they totally agree or not.

CHAPTER TEN
How to Live Your Life Without Becoming a Doormat

In chapter eight, I mentioned that counterpunching was as much to draw a boundary (a consequence) for those who might attack you as it was to 'set the record straight.' This chapter is about that point.

When you consistently allow other people to abuse or mistreat you, it's as if you are saying please "do it more."

I believe the majority of Americans are doormats. They quietly loathe other people and resent them, but they rarely take action to change what they resent the most. They internalize abuse and ultimately become what their abusers want them to be: beaten into submission, weak, apathetic, and resentful.

Abusers ultimately need victims in order to remain relevance and in power. Most of the liberal Democrat platform, in America, is predicated on the fact that there is a victim class and Democrats are there to solve their problems. If anyone tells you they're going to help you solve a problem, the first question you should ask is "how much is it gonna cost me?" In political terms, the cost is everything. The cost is your upward mobility, your dignity, and the American dream. In business terms, the cost usually involves giving away your rights or the ability to profit from your efforts.

I'm not here to decry liberal or Democratic policy. I'm simply making the point that their policies are focused on blaming the causes behind the victims of our society instead of leading victims to overpowering those forces.

Anyone who tells you that you're a victim is attempting to prey on your emotional instability or weakness for their own self- aggrandizement and/ or financial gain. The powerful elites in our society, both in business and politics, need victimized doormats in order to remain relevant and in power.

To be fair, this phenomena exists in both political parties thus why I call myself conservative but not Republican.

Don't be a doormat!

From the moment Trump rode the escalator down to the lobby of Trump Tower to announce his candidacy; I've been awestruck by one particular element of his ascent to the presidency. He is anything but a doormat. It's not just his resolve and confidence, his incredible counterpunching, or his boldness in tackling taboo issues that I find amazing. It's the fact that he's never submissive to the powerful elite who typically and overwhelmingly control their victims and opponents.

Many people decry Trump's style. They call it "unpresidential, demagoguery, bigoted, racist, or xenophobic" and a host of other nasty catchphrases. Trump reminds me a lot of my grandfather. You never questioned where you stood with him. He seemingly had no filter with the things he said. At times, he was outright rude. But, he was as honest as they come and you never were met with unrealistic expectations. Some people would call him a curmudgeon. Others would call him sharp, resolute, and effective.

I've learned never to be affected by the style and delivery of the truth. One of the biggest tragedies of our time is the fraudulent nature and 'fakeness' that surrounds our world. Gone is a propensity toward being genuine. How can I decry Trump's style, even his delivery when transparency and candor are strong qualities he possesses?

 The greatest misfortune of our time is that we have a population of millions of Americans who sit idly and watch the world go by. They do little to change it. They care little about anything but their own material desires. They're apathetic, lazy, and thoughtless.

 I've just described the congregation of many churches in America. Millions of Americans have fallen prey to this high pressure society such that they check the boxes so that they look good but they don't take actions that **are good**.

 I live within a complex of three high-rise condominiums, three major Atlanta office buildings, and one of the largest churches in America: Buckhead Church. I remember a stunning moment following a church service one day as I was walking back to my condo. Four guys were walking out of church and one of them rather brazenly said "f*ck it, I don't give a God-d**m!" There were two to three dozen people in his proximity who seemed stunned. He quickly replied, "oh, I'm so sorry…"

 I'm always challenged in moments like these as to whether I should make a statement or ignore them. I chose the latter because one of his friends punched him and reminded him of where he was.

The point of telling you this is that a church service had just ended and this individual was so consumed by something toxic he didn't realize where he was or had just been. He wasn't in the spirit of church even though he had just left it. He was another 'box-checker.' My guess is that he's a perfect example of someone who would take significant issue with President Trump's style and demeanor. We have a word for that in the English language: hypocrite.

 Hypocrites disgust me. They are the first to take a sanctimonious tone with the rest of society and believe they are anointed as the moral police, while displaying actions that are completely the opposite. Most of the time these are the people that are telling you what is wrong with you. They are doing it to distract from the fact that they are a much bigger culprit of whatever they're considered with you about.

 Recently, my wife joined our homeowner's association (HOA) board of directors. She was elected in a sort of coup which unseated a decade-long board member. Much like our political system many organizations across the country are filled with people who seemingly never leave. They're sanctimonious, self-anointed moral police who crave power. Usually, they are ineffective, destructive, and in some cases illicit. In politics, we call this "the establishment."

 Our HOA still has one board member who has served since the beginning of the association. At the first meeting after my wife was elected, he approached her to have a private discussion about 'her husband': me. He pointed out that she had a higher standard to meet now that she was an elected board member in our HOA. His intention was to try to leverage her position into keeping me quiet on matters that I felt were important. He directly stated that my tone, style, and approach to disagreements in the building, particularly with management and the board itself, would have to change. I'd call this outright bullying.

 She was a bit stunned by this arrogant and conceited diatribe. Frankly, I was angered by it. Had I been present for such a comment I would have looked at him and said "you have been one of the most incompetent and ineffective people in this building since its completion. I will tell you what I think, when I think it, and I will speak my mind when I feel it's appropriate. And if you don't like it, you can kiss my ass."

 A lot of people would call such a response unprofessional, reckless, and certainly bombastic.

It would have been anything but that. What I have found with people like this board member is that most people succumb to their own passive-aggressive bullying. They're not used to being challenged let alone directly put in their place.

 It's rare that Republicans face the kind of harsh attacks and blowback from a fellow primary candidate as did the presidential hopefuls of the 2016 primary. The minute they made passive-aggressive and bullying comments against Trump, he slammed them. As a result, most people were shocked by Trump's reaction and not by the fact that these candidates were picking a fight in an attempt to appear morally superior and demean their opponent. I have always been amazed that it's okay to use sophisticated language in a veiled attempt to sound professional while they're really being deviant and abusive.

 I have no patience for fake people and therefore I believe it's our duty in society to put them in their place each time an opportunity presents itself.

 Because my wife didn't immediately push back and draw a clear boundary with such commentary on the HOA board, the comments and passive-aggressiveness have continued. Had she made a comment similar to the one I described above, that would have been the end of such bullying. She is learning in these situations why my style sometimes seems so crass but is ultimately effective. This is the same reason that Trump has learned to use a crass but effective style in order to battle his opponents.

While some of our citizens become outraged by that style and offended, they are sadly not recognizing that they are living the life of a doormat. Everyone stomps on a doormat and wipes their feet. A doormat is dirty and after a couple of years of abuse is discarded and replaced. We throw old, abused doormats in the trash.

While it may be popular to use sophisticated language and attempt to sound professional at all times, in doing so, you are being a doormat. You will be used and tossed aside in almost everything you do in life. If you don't fight for you, no one else will!

Did you notice the massive army of Americans that fought for Trump on every issue and at all costs? Remember his "Fifth Avenue" comment?

When you refuse to be a doormat, you will be met with accusations of being unprofessional, mean, or even malicious. While this may not be a pleasant reaction, over time, it creates a consequence realized by others for abusing you. It establishes a boundary and it makes people pick their battles with you instead of oppressing you at every chance they get.

Most people go through life wanting to be liked by as many people as possible. I talked about this phenomenon in chapter four. My hypothesis in that chapter was that it's better to be respected than liked.

It's possible to be liked by the overwhelming majority of the people you meet. However, you will likely never make a meaningful difference in their lives or yours. Being liked requires you to be less than honest, avoid candor, run from conflict, and generally not take a stand for your own values. People who are well-liked typically have low integrity. They use situational ethics in order to appeal to the audience in front of them. Since they rarely participate in conflict and avoid being candid they rarely receive the growth and educational benefits of receiving the same.

By contrast, when you seek to engage in conflict for the sake of resolving a problem, you invite people who are threatened by such change to dislike you. This creates 'the other' of our society.

'The other' is the group or person who opposes you because they are forced by you to deal with their problems. To them, you are their 'other.' By fighting for your values and striving to reach your purpose, you will attract people that not only respect you but like you.

'The Others" is the subject of our next chapter, but what does that mean?

CHAPTER ELEVEN
The 'Others'

The title of this chapter makes it sound like we just stepped into a 'sci-fi novel.' While that is not the case, the subject is equally mystical.

Increasingly our lives can be reduced to "us versus them." Some describe this by saying we all seek echo chambers that validate our intrinsic values and beliefs. Americans rarely seek the answer to the valuable question "where could I be wrong?" Instead, we take a position and anyone who opposes that position is 'the other.' They are not only wrong, they are the enemy.

In their world, we are 'the other.'

I am not advocating echo chambers. I'm certainly not advocating believing that you're always right and that everyone who opposes you is always wrong. In reality, I believe the number one secret to long-term success is always asking "where could I be wrong?" then listening for that answer. If you are willing to ask this question and hear the answers (some of which will challenge everything you believe and sometimes change it) without being offended your quality of life will improve dramatically. So will your success.

"Where am I wrong?"

Even if you can become the open minded person I described above, this does not mean the vast majority of our neighbors will. Most people will continue to believe they are right and you're wrong. If you dare challenge them, you are now 'the other,' the enemy. As I stated in the last chapter, the moment you become candid and fight for your beliefs and values is the moment your likability goes way down and overall respect goes up in some cases. If you're like me, you simply don't care.

In heated moments of controversy we have to always remember that our own self-confidence, self-worth, and faith in a higher power is all that matters.

It is not up to the community to judge whether I have broken my own moral code and values. So long as I'm following the law and respecting the ethical guidelines that I have submitted to, the judgment of 'the others' is the most toxic and worthless information I can receive. If I allow it, it will distort my values rob me of my purpose and ultimately damage my moral compass as I attempt to be liked and approved by everyone.

Instead, I view disapproval of my connections as a badge of honor.

In my media career, there's been no shortage of accusations that I'm racist or bigoted. I take that as a compliment. In my heart, I know that I desire the same thing that Martin Luther King Jr. desired during the civil rights movement. Not only do I desire equality, I pray for upward mobility for anyone stuck in poverty. The accusations of being racist or bigoted come when I dare to point out - not only the root causes of generational poverty - but start to cite the demographics that suffer from it the most.

I have experienced a tremendous amount of blowback for being a Trump supporter. Someone very close to me once said, "Bryan I know you well. I know where your heart is and I simply believe you're better than supporting this man. You're better than this: the way he behaves, how he makes fun of people, and how he talks to other people who oppose him."

For the people who know me well, they would laugh to hear that I was speechless.

My first response was simply that "I'm not better than anyone nor do I get the right to judge that." My second reaction was the most meaningful and I'm going to share with you.

My friend was right. I would not typically support a politician as bombastic as Trump. Given the choice (and 10 to 15 years ago), I would have much rather had Vice-President Pence as our president. However, we need the shock and awe that Trump has brought to the Oval Office in order to 'wake us the hell up.'

I see our society as one that has lost its way and in some cases become morally bankrupt. We seem to no longer care about serving our communities and putting our faith and the human condition ahead of our own selfish material desires. Our politicians have taken advantage of our disdain for conflict as a society.

As a result, we allow deep-rooted and powerful politicians to take control of Americans ability to hold its government accountable. We're so afraid of the conflict involved in taking that power back, and the short term costs it may create, we do nothing. We are idle and apathetic as a society. The more conflict they create, the less we have historically paid attention and the more the powers that be get away with it.

How is it possible to change this? First, the people who are least offended by President Trump are likely the people who live their lives by standing up for their beliefs and by engaging in conflict and candor. This includes me. While we may not agree with everything Trump says or does, we're also not offended and concerned by it because were used to it.

By contrast, the people who are most offended by Trump are the people who most represent everything I've described as destroying the fabric of our society. These are the people that get coined 'snowflakes' who need 'safe spaces' where the outside world of conflict and reality doesn't penetrate their distorted and utopian view of it. These people exist on both sides of the political aisle. That explains why there was such a large faction of '#NeverTrump' conservatives (or Republicans) during his ascent to the White House.

In essence, Trump made all of these liberal and conservative snowflakes face the harsh realities they had been avoiding. By doing so, many call him a divisive president. I see it as completely the opposite. He may be one of the most unifying forces this country has ever seen. We just haven't given him time to turn the tide.

Wait!

In case you're snowflake and have made it this far, let me explain. By forcing us to deal with issues we would otherwise avoid we may actually solve them, avoiding the destruction that was lurking under the surface of our discourse. Normally, snowflakes shut down debate through name calling, outrageous emotional breakdowns, and radical false equivalencies. This sort of behavior usually prevails in our discourse because historically politicians who engage in it lose elections.

The social media revolution, combined with Trump's prowess with handling substantial conflict means a different kind of politician and leader can now prevail. Many people in our country felt forgotten before the election of Trump. Whether you agree with his positions or not, he spoke to those people and for them. In doing so, it appeared he was violating every rule of leadership and political success. He appeared to be one of the least liked candidates ever to receive a major party nomination.

When I tell you that being liked doesn't matter and stifles your purpose, I mean it. There are a lot of people that liked Hillary Clinton, but didn't show up to vote for her sorry ass. Accordingly, Trump's constituency added respect to their list of emotional sentiments attached to their candidate. By earning the respect of his community/ supporters, he suddenly created passion for his cause.

Clinton's causes were met with very little passion because people liked her for her positions but disrespected her because of her perceived true convictions. Her positions were in conflict with her past convictions.

What '#NeverTrump' Americans seemingly never realize is that Trump's convictions were simply bringing America back to its exceptionalism or greatness. His entire campaign can be summarized by one slogan "Make America Great Again." An overwhelmingly large number of Americans both liked and respected Trump for being bold enough to speak for them. A similarly large number of Americans didn't like Trump because of his style or comments, but respected him because they agreed with his message. He got both sets of voters: those who just respected him and those who both liked and respected him.

What was Hillary Clinton's message? "Trump is bad... I've served this country my entire life and it's my turn..." Plus, "we just had our first African-American president, so now we need our first female president."

That was an arrogant and selfish message. It was a message delivered by a sanctimonious, self-righteous politician who believed she was morally superior to everyone else. She believed it was her position to judge her opponent and that given her entitlement to the position of president, we should be commanded to listen. Most people saw the messaging as an attempt to manipulate them and to use victim mentality to appeal to voters.

Contrasting these two styles, Trump was telling everyone to stop being victims and to start winning again. Clinton had a message of entitlement that was "you are victim and I'll fix it for you because you can't fix it yourself."

When you reduce the 2016 election to the simple terms and forgo all the controversies and media outbursts, it's very easy to see why Trump won. First, he wasn't a doormat. Second, his constituency was more impassioned by his message than 'the other.' If you haven't connected this, 'the others' were victims who supported

Clinton because they wanted someone to fix their self-created problems.

While we've established that it's never appropriate to believe you're always right and that your opponent is always wrong, you also have to realize that for everything you do, there will always be 'the other.' In politics, there has to be a winner and a loser. In business, there can be multiple winners.

It's fair to say politics is different for that reason alone.

I don't believe in winning at others expense, but I do believe in defeating others who attempted to demean, judge, or defeat me. If someone else is attempting to win at my expense, I better figure out how to make them lose in that effort before I do. This is precisely why being a doormat is a perfect formula for failure.

By always questioning where I could be wrong and also being willing to listen, I have empowered myself to be able to fulfill my purpose, reach my goals, and simultaneously earn the most respect while doing so. Because most of your opponents ('the others') are unwilling to admit where they could be wrong, they will eventually be blindsided by their avoidance of reality. They may be liked in the short term, but in the long run they will be disliked and disrespected as the world around them unravels.

When you know that your intentions are pure (for the good of others and not just yourself), that you hold deep convictions and serve your purpose, stand up and fight for it. Most people fight for selfish causes and accordingly have a hard time with people who are righteous.

Please notice that I say "righteous" and not "self-righteous." There is a substantial difference. Being self-righteous is the process of believing you are morally superior. Righteousness is the state of being morally superior without having to convince anyone that you are. Put another way, self-righteousness is usually being wrong while believing you're better than everyone else. Righteousness is usually being morally right while not realizing you might in fact be behaving in a morally superior fashion.

The righteous almost always receive the most short term criticism and volatility, especially when they engage in conflict and are candid. Sadly, most people are capable of being righteous but refuse to do so because of the short term costs. It's a great tragedy that these people never realize the potential for long term peace, prosperity, and meaningful legacy.

The next time 'the other' side of your argument starts calling you names, listen to their arguments and if there are none, you likely are righteous. The next time 'the other' group starts attacking you, listen to their reasons for the attacks and if there are none, it's probably because you're starting to make a difference.

If they make some valuable points that can challenge your thinking, be willing to listen. Humility is a valuable trait when it's centered in being willing to evolve and grow as a person.

Never allow the attacks to change your convictions, purpose, or God given righteousness. Fight back and win. The future of our society and the legacy for your children depends on it.

CHAPTER TWELVE
The 'Be Nice Crowd'

The title of this chapter is one of my key phrases of life. Without calling it 'the be nice crowd," we've been talking about these people throughout this entire book.

'The be nice crowd' is a group of people who act one way in public and another in private. These are the preachers that cheat on their wives. These are the highly successful businessmen who beat their wives. These are the political pundits in the activist media who spend most of their time bashing people like President Trump. These are the people you first meet at a new job who tell you all the unwritten rules of the workplace. These are the people that quote you a Bible verse the minute you encounter a business conflict with them.

Simply stated, 'the be nice crowd' is the biggest fraud of our society. Some of them are criminals, but most of them are not. They are even worse than criminals.

Criminals engage in a series of illegal and illicit activities that can be detected, most people have a hard time believing that criminals are behaving completely the opposite when no one is looking.

I believe we all have a duty to snuff out these liars and bring them to social justice. Catching criminals is important but so is catching fraudulent and incompetent people and holding them accountable for the damage they cause.

This chapter is so fitting for this book because most people would agree that the public persona of President Trump is anything but nice. In reality, Trump is a rare circumstance where he may actually be much nicer in person than in the public square. If you take an apolitical approach to studying the life of Trump, you find that most people who have worked with him like and respect him. It's the people that barely know him and refuse to study his background that most dislike him.

Bingo! There you have 'the be nice crowd.' This crowd has only one goal: to convince you that they are the moral authority on any subject matter they touch. Generally, they have been successful at doing this.

Their technique is always the same, especially in media. Take something out of context, identify it as being morally wrong (if not also legally wrong), distort reality so that the subject creates fear in the audience, make sure the controversy goes viral so that everyone is talking about it, and then demand an apology. Historically, the media has been able to successfully prevail with this technique for decades. Very rarely does a politician, public figure, or well-known businessperson fight back against the activist media. Instead, they are beaten into submission and succumb to the pressure of the negative publicity to eventually issue an apology.

'The be nice crowd' (re: moral authority) wins again. The loser in this equation is always the person giving the apology. Refer back to chapter four entitled "The Apology Tour" for why apologizing is never a good idea.

From calling illegal immigrants "rapists and murderers" to debating politics with a Gold Star dad to flailing his hands in a debate against a lying but disabled reporter, there has been plenty for 'the be nice crowd' to find wrong with Trump. However, in order for them to win the race for moral superiority, they had to actually obtain the apology. They didn't.

As a result, Trump won and they lost. In the process some of the more respected media talent, politicians, and business leaders have lost a lifetime of honor and respect. Many have quietly disappeared from television like George Will, Bill Kristol, and Erick Erickson from Fox News. Others have become wholly irrelevant. Several politicians like Jeb Bush, Carly Fiorina, and Bobby Jindal, once rising stars in the Republican Party, have virtually vanished from politics. To most of America, the mere mention of their names is met with a negative response even from people who dislike Trump.

'The be nice crowd' would argue that Trump creates the same negative response in a majority of Americans. I would cede that point except I would add that Trump has the largest bully pulpit in the world and ultimately was victorious in attaining the highest and most powerful office known to man. I would also point out that it's never appropriate to judge a leader today. The true test of leadership is that it must stand the test of time and presidents ultimately are best judged two to three decades later. The 'be nice crowd' can't be inconvenienced by these facts or realities.

It is usually safe to assume that when someone approaches you to just give you a 'heads up' or let you know about some arbitrary rule you're breaking, they see you as a threat. Likely, they're doing much worse in that they're trying to get you to stop doing. "I'm just going to tell you," or "I'm just letting you know" precedes a judgment of what you're doing is not in the spirit of helping you.

I typically ignore these fools and idiots. When that passive approach doesn't get them out of my way, then I quietly take mental notes and at the appropriate moment put them in their place.

Yes, they are usually offended, even outraged when I finally draw a boundary and call them out for the frauds they really are, but that's their problem not mine.

What I'm describing in this chapter, you must become keenly able to recognize. It's what Trump did when he pushed back at the ridiculousness and projections against him by evil forces disguised as nice people.

Let me add one final thing. Acting professional is far less important than being professional. If my behavior is cordial and nice (professional) but the manifestation of my actions and efforts is harmful to others, then my result is evil. If my style or demeanor is harsh (unprofessional) but the manifestation of my actions and efforts is helpful and uplifting to others, then my result is good.

Words don't matter. Actions do.

Actually, results matter even more than words and actions.

CHAPTER THIRTEEN
Dealing with Incompetent People

A friend of mine once said to me, in describing a mutual acquaintance, that they were simply "an incompetent person." I had never heard it put that way. Usually 'incompetence' is a word used to describe a behavior or specific inaction or inability. In reality, some people **are** just incompetent at everything.

Incompetent people usually fit in well with 'the be nice crowd.' However, they are not knowingly hiding what they're doing wrong. They're just usually wrong. Sometimes incompetent people are more harmful than criminals or the immorality projected by 'the be nice crowd.' They're more harmful because they have no awareness as to how inept they are. Much like 'the be nice crowd' they're also usually very nice. This is a self-protection mechanism to cover up their incompetence.

Criminals or 'shady people' usually calculate their abuses against others. In an attempt to remain undetected, they rarely cause more harm to others than what is absolutely necessary for their own personal gain. By contrast, incompetent people are not calculated at all. They are reckless, stupid, and ultimately cause even more harm than some criminals and shady people. After all, they don't even know what they don't know.

 Can you imagine a guy as bombastic as Trump who was also incompetent? I realize some people would say I just described President Trump. Wrong! You don't earn billions of dollars and build a substantial and successful business empire by being incompetent. I will let that argument stand on that merit alone.

 The point of asking the question is to point out that most bombastic, colorful people who create controversy are also some of the most competent. Remember, they aren't likable. If you want to be liked, this is not the book for you. If you want to serve your purpose and make a real meaningful difference, keep reading.

 Competence is generally a learned behavior created by situational awareness. Incompetent people are usually lazy. They have little desire to work any harder, learn more, or gain an advantage other than through manipulation. They simply want to maintain what they have with as little effort as possible. Frequently, this means slowing down, getting in the way, or otherwise disrupting competent people's progress.

When a competent person clashes with an incompetent person and begins to point out their deficiencies, this is where the fireworks begin. If you'll recall the Republican primary presidential debates in 2016, they can be summarized by saying it was a debate regarding who was the most competent. As candidate Trump began to make powerful points, the least competent candidates would launch personal attacks. Trump would evaluate those attacks and counterpunch. While you may have disliked his style, this approach is the only way to deal with incompetent people.

We all assume that every person can be reasonable. From an overarching view, this is true. However, when it comes to specific issues such as policy, politics, psychology, or business or taking an analytical view of a deeply rooted problem, incompetent people collapse. They become overwhelmed, feeling exposed for their years of apathy and begin to project their incompetence on the person or group whom they deem is most responsible for their exposure.

In order to find the 'Trump in You,' you have to not only be willing to pursue knowledge, work hard, and make sacrifices, but you have to be willing to counter punch against incompetent people who stand in the way of your purpose and dreams.

Incompetent people are dangerous. They can cost you your livelihood, wreck your marriage, and destroy your reputation.

These people are plentiful in the real estate industry. I spent years in utter amazement as I watched well respected real estate agents negligently serve their clients while projecting a righteous mantra. They were both destructive and situationally delusional at the same time.

In business, incompetence manifests itself mostly in how people "feel" about a contract or procedural guideline. In the midst of a negotiation, they become too overwhelmed to read the policy manual or the legally binding contract. Their emotions tell them that their feeling is correct and that the contract or written material is wrong. They began to argue from a self-righteous standpoint.

One of the most simplistic examples of this in the real estate industry is the 'free refrigerator.' As a sales incentive, it's common that a seller will offer the refrigerator for free in the multiple listing service. Enter the incompetent buyer's agent. Their buyer loves the home and decides to write an offer that is less than full price. They negotiate several items that are not in the seller's original offering. As incompetent agents do, they forget important things like including the refrigerator in the written and legally binding contract.

Fast forward to closing day. The buyer is doing their final walk-through to make sure the home is in order just before closing. They discover the refrigerator is gone. The buyer, being inexperienced in real estate contracts, doesn't realize that their agent should have put the refrigerator in the contract. Since they didn't, the seller decided to remove the refrigerator and sell it to someone else. This is completely justified because the buyer didn't offer full price and negotiated several other terms.

Instead of accepting responsibility, the incompetent buyer's agent begins to attack and yell at the seller's agent. After all, "it's just wrong to offer something like a free refrigerator and then not throw it in at the end under any set of circumstances." The incompetent agent doesn't understand negotiation and they have no desire to. Confronted with the possibility they've made yet another monumental mistake, they're too incompetent to learn from it. Therefore, they appoint blame elsewhere.

There's nothing earth shattering in my refrigerator scenario, it's just an easy example. Incompetent people harm their clients in dozens of ways in almost every transaction. They dispense inaccurate advice based upon feelings and not reality. They omit important protections from contractual language. They unwittingly and grossly misrepresented facts that are instrumental in their clients and customers' decisions. And, they frequently remain undetected as the culprit, because they are so nice.

They are so nice and self-righteous, they cannot detect, under any circumstances, just how dangerous they are.

Think about it! They know how to use all the right professional language with the most submissive and empathetic tone while remaining apathetic and incompetent as hell. While most of their activity is not criminal, in some ways, they are as damaging as any criminal.

I used to believe that being brash, bold, and candid with these people was preying on weakness. I now see it as a fiduciary duty to the people I serve and the business interests I must protect.

Because Trump needed to differentiate himself from less competent and incompetent Republican candidates, he had to tell the audience as such. The reaction by the 'incompetent people' always seemed more professional and righteous because being perceived as morally superior was all they had to offer. The key word here is "perceived." Shattering that perception is an important role when you compete, in any way, with incompetent people or you will be defeated. In reality, Trump deals with his competitors, as president, much in the same way.

Generally, competent people tend to prefer competing with other competent people. This usually becomes a battle of the best sales pitch, the best political ideas, or the best business model. It's rarely a battle of who can personally attack the other the best. Clearly the competent people always win the latter and it's boring. Competent people love challenges and they love to be challenged by other competent people. Moreover, the reward for victory by a competent person against another is far greater then yet another defeat of an incompetent person.

Winning elections, sealing a business deal, or participating in any other initiative against an incompetent person is less about winning and more about not getting destroyed in the process.

This book is entitled the "Trump in You" because Trump is a winner. This book is not a roadmap to winning at others expense. It simply an account of why one of America's most astonishing victories happened and why there's a little bit of that capability in you and likely, a lot.

With that clarity I say this: Run away from incompetent people in your life. Become an expert at detecting those people by keying in on the signs I've outlined. If you can't run away from them, expose them.

Incompetent people are like leeches. They will latch into you and suck life's blood from your body. Successful people never allow this to happen.

CHAPTER FOURTEEN
Closet-Trumpers Theory

 This was my favorite subject throughout the 2016 elections. It was my hypothesis as to why Donald Trump was going to be victorious and become the 45th president of the United States.

For my 10th wedding anniversary, I took my wife to the Ritz-Carlton in St. Thomas, US Virgin Islands. We had been there a few times, and it's one of the most beautiful resorts and settings in the world. I coined the phrase 'Closet-Trumpers Theory' after sitting in a hot tub one night with my wife and another couple from North Carolina we had never met before.

 Oddly, we started talking about politics. As usual, I reserve my political persuasions at the onset of the conversation, so that I can have the privilege of hearing others. I could tell the couple was holding back. They seemed incredibly neutral, likely trying to figure out what was safe to say. After a few minutes, I decided to give them permission to be favorable regarding Trump. Once I did, their praise for him as a presidential candidate started to gush out.

They believed he was exactly what this country needed, someone to 'stir up' the Washington D.C. establishment and force accountability in an otherwise unaccountable and bloated federal government. This was their take - not mine even though I agreed with them.

I had dozens of experiences like this during the election season. They all took the same trajectory: unknown person was hesitant to admit their adoration for Trump until I gave them permission. 'Permission' was simply saying something that made them feel comfortable I would not attack them for being pro Trump.

I estimated that there were 10-20 million 'Closet-Trumpers' that might vote during the 2016 election. It turns out that number was accurate. It was those hidden, 'closet' voters that brought Trump victory and shattered the reputations of the pollsters.

I tell you about this 'theory' so you can understand a key component of success. Sometimes what appears to be the verdict about you in the community isn't real. Frequently, the media and public 'noise' regarding a subject, policy, or person is not representative of the true sentiment of the entire population.

Most people are afraid to fight for what's right. Most people fail to find or live their purpose because they are afraid of the ridicule or criticism that doing so attracts. Winners like Trump are the opposite. They welcome it. They understand that if the media is against them, the people are more likely for them. If the critics are 'extra-polarized' against you, the citizenry is likely equally as polarized in your favor. When your cause is righteous (but not self-righteous), the criticism and ridicule is almost always more vigorous than seeking popular approval. Never allow this reality to confuse you as you fight for a righteous cause yet receive hatred and discord as a result. People who are threatened by your righteous efforts are the first and most vigorous to attack. Always stay the course and you will win the battle. Most people cave under the pressure of being attacked and never realize the power of a righteous cause in the long-run.

I'm reminded of the Warren Buffett investment mentality. Buffet is well known for making radical business decisions through acquisitions and investments that don't make sense. For years he's been one of the five richest men in the world. Why?

Buffet never lets research or polling for popular opinion be his guide. He never lets the so-called 'experts' in the industry tell him how to invest. He always trusts his gut. When he is considering an investment or purchasing a company, he puts more stock in his view of senior management than of expert analysis of the company's stock.

Investing in stocks is a process of looking into the future and determining based upon current circumstances, leadership, and innovation how well the company will fare against competitors. When Wall Street experts tell us that Apple is struggling, I don't buy or sell on that news. I visit the store and see how many people are in the store and how many are leaving with product. It only takes a few visits to see that people are camping out in longer lines for the latest iPhone to realize that last quarter's reports were the past and are not reflective of what the next quarter's are going to be.

The point here is that it's usually what most people don't notice that is an indicator of future results. When 15,000 seat arenas are full across the country, with as many people waiting outside, to see Donald Trump, no poll can accurately reflect what people are thinking; let alone what they will do. Sometimes finding the truth in a culture of puffery, lies, agenda, and fake news is as simple as listening more and saying less.

 I'm reminded of the weekend following the bombshell reveal of a secret recording of Donald Trump with reporter Billy Bush on the 'Access Hollywood' bus. This is the moment that we heard a tape of the two engaged in locker room talk about kissing women and groping them (re: "grab her by the pussy"). I asked my publicist that weekend what he thought. As a Trump supporter, he replied "we're f**ked!" I wasn't so sure.

 I talked to a number of people that weekend in order to gauge an accurate sense of what people were thinking.

 Following the 'Access Hollywood' incident women came forward and began saying Trump had an inappropriate moment with them. It seemed a lot of people questioned the veracity of the claims by at least a couple of these women. Even more concerning was the timing. I keyed in on Jessica Leeds who struck me as a very professional presenter. In fact, she sounded like a professional broadcaster as she eloquently told her story of how Trump groped her on an airplane in first class in the late 1970s.

While I always pause before questioning someone who claims to be a victim of assault, I couldn't shake the feeling that this particular story wasn't believable. I called the Delta Museum in Atlanta, searched all flight records, and spoke to a few aviation experts. I determined that Trump and Leeds flew on an airplane that had non movable armrests in first class. In other words, the eloquent way Leeds described Trump's assault couldn't have happened unless he broke the armrest.

With this discovery, I called my dad and asked him what my mom thought about all of it. I believe the exact quote was that she thought "it is a bunch of BS." At that moment, I realized the 'Access Hollywood' tapes would have no effect on the presidential election. In fact, I think the way these events were presented actually helped Trump even more.

In the age of social media and rapid communication, polls no longer reflect how people **will** behave. They only reflect the feeling at the time the poll is conducted. That's assuming that the poll is reflective of the people who will actually vote. In fact, polls have become more agenda driven than predicted. What I mean is that the pollsters have a bias and they want to use their polls to influence the outcome of an election, event, or cultural belief.

Many pollsters are part of 'the be nice crowd' in that they are resting on their laurels and so called professionalism while working to influence people's psyches and change outcomes. Historically, pollsters were in the business of predicting outcomes.

The American people have a new found suspicion surrounding the media, pollsters, and politicians. There's always been a degree of suspicion, but it's now off the charts. Because of this, some Americans will tell the pollster what they think the popular answer is which may be in direct conflict with their actual position or intended action. In other cases, because sample sizes are so small, people just lie in order to distort the poll.

We've seen this phenomenon in radio broadcasting ratings. The heritage radio station with the most brand recognition always seemed to be favored before digital monitoring for ratings became popular.

Nielsen is the leader in radio broadcasting ratings and sampling. Historically, they used a written diary system for listeners to report radio listening.

In many cases, using diaries, listeners gave credit for all of their listening to their favorite station.

 In 2010, Nielsen launched the people meter, a digital monitoring device of what people actually hear. Almost immediately, the ratings dynamic began to shift. Less popular stations became more popular and some very popular stations lost significant ratings.

 This rating scenario is different than polling for politics. This gives insight into how Americans think. They remember what is most memorable. They act upon what is most actionable. In many cases, people are listening to one radio station less than another but giving credit to the one that is most memorable even if least listened to.

 The lesson is that what seems the best is not always the best and what seems the worst is not always the worst. Perception does count. More importantly, being the most memorable allows you to frame the conversation and control it.

 Trump was attacked and ridiculed more than any presidential candidate in American history. He also responded in kind and showed he was a fighter. When attacks are met with apologies, as outlined in chapter four ("The Apology Tour"), failure is on the horizon. Instead, Trump fought back. Most people do the opposite and hide from the attacks, cave under the pressure, or internalize the negativity.

By fighting back against his critics, he was able to expose some of them as longtime frauds, part of 'the be nice crowd.' In other cases he was able to prove his point by manipulating his critics into contradicting themselves. At times, the critics were exposed for being nothing more than Trump haters without any meaningful substance to their arguments.

Obviously, if you were a Hillary supporter, you said exactly the opposite. This is perfectly acceptable because Trump had already written off swaying any votes from Hillary to his camp.

Most people believe that winning (in politics, policy, or position) is the process of getting an overwhelming majority of people to agree with you. It's not! Winning is getting 50% of the relevant people to agree with you plus one. That's a majority.

In order to be successful, you have to accept that we are a very divided society. We're divided on politics, sports, religion, fiscal policy, income, geography, and so many other issues. I have accepted these realities throughout my real estate career.

 I recognize that I'm a conservative, patriotic American who generally despises the tenets of liberalism. I have friends who are liberal and I understand their positions. But those are exceptions and not the norm for me. I also understood that I'm an outspoken critic on business, religious, cultural, and political matters. Thus, I would damage my real estate business by revealing my public sentiments on those matters.

 Common wisdom is that when you're running a business you stay out of issues of religion and politics. However, common wisdom is 'sheep mentality.' The spirit of such wisdom is that being polarizing on certain issues will limit your appeal for attracting new clients. On the surface, this is true. In reality, this idiotic belief is based upon the idea that 100% percent of the people are your potential clients.

 In every industry, this creates fake people pretending to be apolitical, areligious, asexual, or loosely translated, apathetic. The push is to be neutral on everything. The reality is that you also become ineffective as well.

I took a different approach. I decided to tell the community exactly who I am. I would bare all of my political, religious, and cultural beliefs. I would give strong opinions and produce compelling content. I would use my skills in radio to act as a consumer advocate. I would appeal to the people who believe the country was becoming corrupt. They believed our government was already corrupt. I would present a Christian message with a strong fiscally-conservative set of beliefs. I would narrow my audience and potential list of clients from 100% to just 50%.

Instead of being another option in a sea of people, I became the only option in the pond. Loosely translated, it's better to be a big fish in a small pond that a small fish in a vast ocean. Most people strive for the opposite.

My 'closet-Trumpers theory' proved true because more Americans saw Trump as a transparent, genuine person instead of another politician with policies and positions given to him by a pollster.

Many of the incompetent critics will argue that Hillary Clinton won the popular vote by 3 million. Such an argument represents loser mentality because elections are only based upon popular vote at the state level. I could make my point by rebutting that Trump won 2,623 counties to Clinton's 489, but I'd still be making a loser argument. In reality, Trump won the electoral vote 304 to Clinton's 227.

Losers always try to find victories in their losses. Losing is losing no matter how wide or thin a margin. Losers become winners by focusing on what they did wrong and correcting it. Don't ever forget that.

Finding the 'Trump in You' is easy. Don't listen to the noise of society. Use polling and research only as a guide, not your instruction manual. Trust your gut. Look at the signs that matter, not what so-called 'experts' with competing agendas tell you. Be genuine. Reveal your 'true-self.' Don't let business coaches tell you to become something you're not for the sake of attracting more approval and clients. Understand that if your actions are righteous (but not self-righteous) that you will first garner more criticism than support. Stick to what you believe is right. When you lose, learn lessons about why YOU lost and don't make those mistakes again.

CHAPTER FIFTEEN
Hold No Grudges

One of the most damaging obstacles to your success may lie in holding grudges.

As I am writing this chapter, President Trump has just endorsed former presidential candidate Mitt Romney (R-UT) for Senate. You may recall that Romney gave a series of demeaning speeches calling Trump "a phony" and "a fraud" during the campaign. Trump responded by calling Romney a "choke artist" for losing to President Obama in 2012.

Shortly after Trump's election, he interviewed Romney for a potential appointment to be Secretary of State. Many Trump supporters were unnerved by this because of the attacks Romney launched against Trump as a Republican nominee. Trump doesn't hold grudges. This may be easy for him given that he usually prevails in these public fights.

We see this frequently in politics where two bitter rivals end up becoming seemingly allies in the halls of Congress or the White House. Florida Senator Marco Rubio, South Carolina Senator Lindsey Graham, and Texas Senator Ted Cruz were all engaged in a war of words against Trump. In most cases, they are now working together on the same policies and positions as Republicans.

How can grown men attack each other's families, backgrounds, and personas and then a year later seemingly 'bury the hatchet' and work seamlessly together as allies? They don't internalize the attacks as personal for long. While there may be an initial reaction to take disagreement as a personal attack, you have to let it go. Successful politicians and businessmen learn to do this more rapidly than the rest of us can understand.

As a Trump supporter, you might think that I'm disappointed he endorsed Romney for Senator. I'm not. In fact, I'm impressed by it. Before policy positions, I believe competent leadership is the most important. Romney is an accomplished businessman with an incredible family and a clean record. He has a marvelous wife and a well-adjusted family. While I'm not quick to judge an individual because of their children's problems, I do think it's fair to judge an individual with five children who are incredibly successful and stewards of the community. That's Mitt and Ann Romney. Likely, Trump looks past the personal attacks because of this very fact too.

While Trump may seem anything but humble, the ability to not hold grudges and to befriend former enemies is the essence of humility. In fact, it's necessary for success.

More than anything, Trump may simply recognize the reality of Utah politics expecting Romney to win. Recognizing that you can accomplish more where they agree, he extended 'the olive branch.' Notice there was very little coverage of this humble approach by Trump. We'll hear more about the times that he fights back than when he brings peace. That's okay! We've already established that most of the noise from the media and political class is worthless garbage to us anyway.

If Romney wins, I expect there to be disagreements. The media maggots will focus on those moments much more than when there are agreements. They will do so to highlight a false narrative the Trump gets along with no one. Again, this is loser mentality.

Conflict amongst friends and enemies is the greatest opportunity for growth you will ever discover. If you listen, you hear unfiltered feedback that is delivered in a hurtful way but may reflect how others feel but refuse to admit. While you may need to defend against those attacks in the moment to maintain credibility amongst your followers/customers, you can later reflect on how to adjust in order to prevent similar, future criticisms. Notice that the important aspect is to defend your reputation with your followers not those that are already against you.

 The only way to turn those who hold grudges against you into favoring you is to earn their respect by producing the results they do not believe you can. Even then, you're not likely to turn a majority of your opponents in your favor. But remember it only takes a few more people to maintain a majority of support. And it only takes 50%, plus one, for victory.

 Holding grudges prevents you from learning lessons. Every public disagreement or relationship breakdown has two offending sides. Each side believes their belief is the prevailing and accurate one. Generally, only one can truly prevail.

 This point is critical when you look at the typical American marriage. One of the most toxic and high profile divorces of the 20th century was that of Trump and his first wife Ivana Trump. It was bitter and embarrassing for all involved. Even worse, their three children were the biggest victims.

In the end, Ivana and Donald became lifelong friends and effective parents for their three children Eric, Don Jr. and Ivanka. All three are well-adjusted, successful, disciplined, and responsible. While President Trump gives most of the credit to Ivana, the reality is that both parents decided to forgive each other and not hold a grudge for the ultimate benefit of their children. As a result, and regardless of your view of them as individuals, they succeeded.

Finding the 'Trump in You' is about finding a way to forgive those people who most harm you and let go of grudges while not forgetting their infractions may appear again. I'm not suggesting naïveté here. Conflict will happen and it can be very productive for a short period of time. However, I'm suggesting that if you're in politics or a business industry with enemies, you have to find a way to eventually create peace even if the other party refuses. If not, nothing will get done.

A lot of enemy relationships are created when incompetent people, 'the be nice crowd' or criminals feel threatened by someone who's far more accomplished than they are. They attack not expecting an even more significant counterattack. Most people don't defend themselves. In fact most Americans live in a perpetual world of being beaten into submission.

In many cases, you can't fully escape these people because they're in the same industry or group as you. You have to find a way to extend 'an olive branch' of peace while understanding they're going to continue to be the same incompetent or underhanded people they have always been.

You can remain prepared to recycle the battle with some of these people but holding on to grudges is a cancer that will eat away at your success.

The moral of this chapter is to always look for the good in people while recognizing the evil that prevails in our world. By the way, don't let your guard down. Just don't stay in fight mode all the time with people who have offended you. Forgive them quickly, but don't forget what they did. Let it go and only recycle the battle if they make it unavoidable.

That's exactly where Trump's head is and why he endorsed Romney.

CHAPTER SIXTEEN
Controlling Your Image

Given the context of the last two chapters, it's important we talk about image in this one.

In the last chapter, I briefly mentioned that you sometimes have to defend against attacks in the moment while later reflecting or evolving your beliefs as a result. This is an example of controlling your image.

One of the most dangerous things to do is to allow the perception to prevail that a random critic can instantaneously change your position. Sometimes criticism may become enlightenment and you will change. However, if you allow this to become apparent you will invite even more unwarranted attacks.

Many of Trump's critics loathe the fact that he doesn't apologize, doesn't always seem to have complete facts, and is sometimes believed to be lying. I believe Trump is anything but a liar. However, I do believe at times he is misguided. When he presents a version of facts that he believes to be true but aren't, that doesn't make him a liar. When critics attack him as 'a liar,' his immediate reaction is to counterpunch. This is a necessary response to personal attacks. Controlling your image is incredibly important. Admitting publicly that you're wrong or your position is based upon distorted facts serves no one but your enemies. The only thing that matters is being right in the end.

The reason Trump doesn't always seem to have the full details of a situation in context is likely because details are boring and useless. Many of the 'bad actors' we've discussed in this book (political elites, 'be nice crowd,' some professors, etc) believe that filling their brain with useless factoids somehow creates superiority. What good is all of that information if you don't actually do anything with it. Trump is a doer. 'Doers' usually do things, but frequently miss certain bits of information or facts, that 'do-nothings' and critics believe they should never do.

People like Trump sometimes skim over details that create beliefs that are skewed from what they might actually believe if they had all of the facts. If this means you need to evolve quickly, then so be it.

A person's image is their platform. It's their credibility. Without your credibility and platform, most of what you do and say is meaningless. Here are some examples:

In August 2017 the country was rocked by riots and demonstrations in Charlottesville, Virginia. Most of these demonstrations were by Neo-Nazis, white supremacists, and other bigots. There was an outbreak of violence, and one counter-protester was murdered by a white supremacist who mowed her down with a car.

In the wake of these tragic events, President Trump held a press conference where he said that there "were good people on both sides." He refused to allow the media and political operatives to frame the narrative that this event was all white supremacists versus the African-American population. Such a comment was rooted in the fact that many people at the event were there to protest the removal of Confederate monuments and were not part of the white supremacist or neo-Nazi groups.

This is another example of what seems to be popular (as presented by the media) but really isn't. The media created an impression that made it taboo to say anything publicly other than what they sanctimoniously felt was appropriate. As a result, this silenced many Americans who agreed with Trump's controversial statements.

Missing from the conversation was the fact that Antifa (a violent, racist, and bigoted anti-white group) incited a lot of the violence. That was an inconvenient fact the media did not want its apathetic audience to hear. They simply wanted Trump to denounce everyone at the event as bigots and racists, and if not, they wished to frame him in those same terms.

As of this writing, he still has refused to take that bait.

It may seem that his failure to comply and agree with the media had the opposite of the intended effect on Trump's image. Let's look deeper. Remember, it's easy to gain credibility in the media by bashing Trump. It's nearly impossible to gain any by supporting him. This dynamic has created a visual that "it's popular to bash the president." By contrast, "it's damaging to publicly support him." As a result, we only hear one side of the view point.

But, who is lurking in the crowd of voters that agree with Trump and his supporters and are simply silent about it because they are afraid of the type of backlash the media has displayed against Trump and his supporters consistently? The answer is millions of people.

Additionally, Trump is not trying to actually win the approval of those that oppose him. He is simply trying to remain credible with his base of supporters. By caving to the media, he gains no one and loses those who are most important to his platform. Millions of Americans silently supported his realistic view of the events of Charlottesville. Their voices were not heard because they were afraid of the backlash they would receive or they were not given equal time by media to present their view.

Trump understands this. He also understands that the media is now much more than cable news, printed newspaper, and the nightly news networks. In fact, most of his supporters get their news from Fox News, social media, or by watching unedited (in context) media on platforms like YouTube. They have learned that the media can edit the reality or context of any event too easily and therefore are not influenced by their presentations or opinions any longer.

Over time, feeling that they had won the argument in the hearts and minds of their viewers/

audiences, the media will continue to default to the same approach they took in Charlottesville. As a result, moderate American voters begin to clearly see the lies and distortions by our media and recognize that Trump may, in fact, be more accurate than the media has portrayed. This would not be possible if Trump caved to the demands of the media.

In order to control your image, it is sometimes necessary to do the opposite of what most people think you should do. Sometimes you have to attract extremely negative blowback in order to have the opportunity to make your point heard.

Recently, in our HOA I sent what was deemed a very nasty and unprofessional email pointing out that our management was incompetent. I added that they love to police residents in pursuit of perfect behavior while dropping the ball on a number of their most basic job descriptions. I further added that I thought it was "shitty" to hold us to perfect accountability while being so far off the mark themselves. I continued that I believe they see their role as one requiring them to be punitive to the residents that own here as opposed to being supportive. Honestly, I added a curse word or two because I knew its likely effect.

Was I professional in my approach? No, not according to 'the be nice crowd!' However, out of a host of issues, this style immediately elevated mine to the most discussed. What I have found, unfortunately, is that a professional response to a repeated and unending problem tends to continue being ignored.

My statements were met by a board member stating how unprofessional my email was and how I was being abusive to the manager who 'dropped the ball.' I call it holding him accountable since no one else will. My email sparked a chat amongst the board members which ultimately resulted in the problem being solved.

While I don't enjoy having to make harsh statements and send nasty emails, they are effective. Usually, I first try to reason with individuals in matters of conflict. After several attempts, I either decide to pick my battles and drop the issue altogether or to plant 'a verbal bomb' for the sake of an emotional reaction by the other side. When my apathetic opponent won't be reasonable, I have to spur their emotions somehow to cause them to care even if they retaliate against me. Adding a little fear and pain into a subject tends to get people off their lazy asses and into action.

As a result, when I'm dealing with a customer service issue or debate over beliefs, when I'm met with the phrases "let's keep this professional" or "please control your language," I know I'm making progress.

When an otherwise apathetic person, unwilling to be reasonable begins to be affected by my lack of professionalism or language I'm finally giving them a reason to care. Translated, this means it's now more painful to be apathetic to my cause that actually do something to make things right.

Avoiding conflict is one of the most dangerous aspects to your image. Without conflict you rarely get more than a fleeting second to make a point. Because of the appetite for conflict in America, we gain far more attention when we are passionately debating our beliefs than we do when we simply state them professionally and calmly in hopes that someone hears them.

To believe it's appropriate to make every presentation, position, or assertion in an arbitrarily defined "professional manner" is delusional. The highest rated shows on television are 'reality shows." These are almost all conflict based because the American people find it entertaining.

Why would I deny them the same entertainment on an issue I care about the most? If it's not presented in a way that creates emotion, it's usually ineffective.

 You may not agree with Trump or his statements involving Charlottesville. However, his response sparked a two-week long and meaningful discussion about race that this country hasn't had in decades. By caving to the media demands requiring appointing blame and guilt in Charlottesville, we may have been spared the entire backlash. However, we benefited from the conversation. Trump knew it and that explains his response.

 Controlling your image is not always about gaining popular consensus and appearing perfect. Sometimes it's about creating a scenario that sparks a meaningful debate that you know is desperately needed to solve the problem.

 There's another way to describe this: leadership. In many cases, your image as a leader is best served not by how you are viewed in an immediate sense but over a long span of time.

 To those who believe they can predict how President Trump's legacy will actually turn out should immediately go buy a lottery ticket and pick all of the numbers themselves because they are smarter than everyone else. No one can predict the future, but many people arrogantly do it with Trump. Accordingly, they are setting themselves up to fail by doing so.

CHAPTER SEVENTEEN
Reaching for a Purpose Bigger Than Yourself

I laugh every time I hear an 'expert pundit' say Trump never really wanted to be president. Such a statement makes about as much sense as saying a fish never really wants to be in the water.

There's incompetence to such a statement because it's a small minded way of explaining something that a loser will never understand.

Trump was probably bored running his company. Regardless of your financial desires, no amount of monetary success is sufficient. Everyone is wired to want something bigger than themselves.

This chapter speaks to 'purpose.' We're all born with innate talents and personality traits. Our biggest challenge is tapping into those. Another challenge we face is being able to do what we love and monetize it for survival and even wealth.

People like Trump who were fortunate enough to find their life's passion, eventually grow tired of the financial success. You don't have to be a billionaire to find this reality. You just have to have been blessed enough to be doing what you love in life, as a career, while making great money doing it. Eventually, you will decide that another zero on your bank account or a new jet does not add any more happiness or fulfillment. You reach a point where you feel like you owe the world something more.

In most cases, this is a very humble moment where you realize that most of what you've been doing was about you (and maybe your family) but hasn't necessarily made a lasting difference on society.

For most of us, the result of this revelation is akin to going on a mission trip, working as a volunteer for charity, or organizing a community group for underprivileged children. In these cases we touch dozens, maybe hundreds of lives in a positive way. Needless to say, it doesn't take more than a few hundred thousand of us doing those things to change society and the world.

For a rare few, becoming president is a whole new universe. Most incredibly successful people are not successful because of their pursuit of money. They are successful because they pursued a career they love. Inevitably, after years of material success, most people are presented with a calling to do something even greater, especially billionaires like Trump.

If you look at Trump's personal balance sheet, combined with his high-profile celebrity status, he didn't need the attention or power that comes with being president. He already commanded the attention of almost every television network on demand. He's amassed a fortune that will sustain him, his children, and their children into eternity. But, why did so many people believe Trump simply wanted the attention that running for president would garner?

The people who believe he really didn't want to win are people who are so selfish and self-absorbed by their own self-aggrandizement that they couldn't possibly understand a selfless act by another person. That's the only way to explain it.

I believe Trump saw flaws in our government resulting from years of having to deal with it on his development projects. While he was successful at doing so, he also likely found the process disgusting.

While I've only experienced a fraction of the success of Trump, I do understand the resentments that form after years of having to succumb to and play the system. 'The System' is a general reference to idiotic industry standards or government regulations that stand in the way of smart business decisions.

When you're running a multimillion dollar company (or multibillion) and the last approval needed to execute a project is being handled by government bureaucrat earning $60,000 a year, it's demoralizing. In saying this, I'm not trying to demean government workers. I'm simply pointing out that many of them are corrupted by the power and the ego boost they gain from having control over multimillion or multibillion dollar projects and companies. How can someone on a government salary earning $60,000 possibly do the best job of handling government's intentions and help a business at the same time? They can't.

As Trump stated during the election, most politicians of national prominence have come to him for a campaign donation at one point or another. He made a joke out of the fact that they would get 'down on their knees' begging for money if he had asked. He explained to the American people that the reason he was the right candidate is that he had been using the system to his favor for years and believed it was stacked against most of us.

When Trump made those statements, I connected to them in a deep and meaningful way. After years of serving in volunteer-roles in the National Association of Realtors and specifically as a member of the Board of Directors of a local Association, I saw firsthand how successful agents were abused and dismissed and below average agents were supported. This is a microcosm of government and our business community as well.

I call it the race to average. Industry trade organizations, state governments, and our federal government all promote average and below average business behavior. This means that losers are given a chance to be average without any meaningful effort and winners constantly struggle to maintain their success because of the onslaught of attacks and assaults to promote the average. We have literally become a culture and a country that penalizes success.

Powerful and established business people can overcome this punitive culture because of their deep connections to government officials, elected officials, and the business community. However, the smartest minds and talents of the 21st century don't have the same opportunity as they did in the last century. Once you devise a business plan that solves the problem and threatens to be disruptive, government or industry establishments began to fight for the status quo. In some cases our government has weaponized its operations for political purposes instead of serving the American people.

I've often said that the success I realized as a real estate salesperson and broker would be nearly impossible, even given my work ethic and talent, in 2018 versus when I started 20 years ago. Things have changed. If you find a better way to do something, it's no longer rewarded. In the age of YouTube and social media, everyone believes they're an expert. Therefore, the true experts, are no longer revered and rewarded. They are chastised for their threat to the status quo and for the potential of causing others to have to work harder to maintain their current achievements. This is disgusting and is an existential threat to the future success of our country.

How many more buildings can Trump build and still feel the reward and accomplishment as he did with the first few? I can assure you that the Trump Tower, where Trump owns a $100 million penthouse still gives him as much pleasure when he walks through the doors as the groundbreaking ceremony of some new 70 story high-rise. But at some point, you realize there's something more you are called to do.

This explains why Trump ran for public office for the first time at nearly 70 years old. He saw the atrocities of business and the struggles that others face in today's America that in no way resembles the America that paved the path for his great success.

Winners like to win when competing against other winners. Beating or winning against a bunch of losers is not rewarding. Remember, the kind of success that Trump has realized never comes out of the pursuit of money and prestige. Those two things may come with the territory, but they are symptoms not the cause. The cause was his passion and drive that resulted from doing something he loves (real estate development).

I have always described my real estate career as a passion and purpose for helping people make the toughest financial decisions they face. I was damn good at it. I still am. I could take the most complicated foreclosure, job loss, or seemingly inevitable bankruptcy situation and solve it. While that may have involved my client selling a house and doing a short sale, it also involved me helping them save their financial ass. I never saw my job as getting paid for selling houses. My job and career was helping people make decisions that would better their financial lives and as a result I would get paid for it most of the time.

Most people pursue the commission at the end of the sale. For them, it's that simple. They pursue the profit after they flip a real estate deal. They pursue the paycheck at the end of the week. They never live in the moment. They just live for the payoff. I've learned to live in the moment, enjoying more of the process of making money as opposed to the receipt of the money. You can only find peace in your life when you enjoy what you do every day. The minute you start to loathe getting up and going to work is the minute you are no longer serving your purpose. You are serving your master, which is usually money, a horrible boss, or both.

No matter how much you love what you do, at some point you need a bigger challenge. No matter how much money you can make doing what you do, at some point, the money doesn't matter anymore.

We've seen this phenomenon with Bill Gates the founder of Microsoft. I think it's fair to say he loves the company he created but no longer loves working in it day-to-day. He took his vast fortune, approaching $100 billion, and has set out to give it away to help cure AIDS and disease in impoverished Third World countries. He's used his influence and power amongst other billionaires to invite them to do the same. Gates is well on his way to creating a philanthropic society with $1 trillion worth of influential power as a tool to make the world a better place. Does anyone think he's doing this because of the prestige, money, or power it creates? He's not.

Then why do people think that Trump running for president, using tens of millions of his own dollars is any different? It's not.

Trump created a byproduct of his success that very few people do. He created a billion-dollar earned media empire. What I mean by this is that Trump has the power to say something and garner enough free media attention (earned media) that eclipses what any Fortune 500 company could even buy in advertising. I could write an entire book about this phenomenon, and I may. However, what's important is to understand that you can create a small version of this for yourself and your local community.

While I can't tell you how to specifically do it to fit your personality and style, I can share with you my story. When I left the radio business for a brief six months in the year 2000 to focus on my burgeoning real estate career, I was looking for a new way to do an old job: housing sales.

A former colleague of mine had just gotten into sales at a conservative talk radio station in Charleston, South Carolina. He suggested I start hosting a weekend real estate show on their talk station. Obviously, this was a sales pitch, but a damn good one. I wasn't out of radio for six months before I got back in the business.

Years later, I would realize that I never really exited the radio and media business. I simply found a new way to monetize it. The way I describe it now is that I've been a radio host since 1994 and that for a period of 16 years I made most of my money selling real estate to people I met through the radio station airwaves. Most of my clients were radio listeners.

After the first few years of hosting the real estate show, I realized that people really didn't want to hear about how to prepare their home to be sold or who had the best mortgage rates in town. People really wanted to hear stories that reflected their experiences in the real estate business. They wanted to know how we think, why we do some of the things that we do, and how we get away with it as an industry. Come to think of it, this is what drove me into the industry in the first place. My first two Realtors were wonderful people but the process of buying my first two homes was a living nightmare. I thought I could do better.

 In many cases I did do better. It wasn't so much that I could make the process any more pleasurable. It was that I made more realistic expectations. More importantly, I would talk about the infractions, the illegal activity, or the abuses that I saw on a regular basis in the industry. My audience loved it!

 At one point I took on Bank of America for what I believed was absolutely mortgage fraud. To their credit, by the writing of this book, it seems they have cleaned up their act greatly. Bank of America's big mistake was buying Countrywide Mortgage. It would not be a stretch to say Countrywide could be called the most responsible for destroying the financial markets of the United States of America. As with most of my audience, I was stunned no one at Countrywide went to jail for what they did. Why would they? Eric Holder, then Attorney General of the United States, worked for the banks before he was appointed to that post and now works for them again. Explaining the unexplainable became my radio show.

I became the person who would challenge the Association of Realtors for being unethical (while it was charged with being the ethics police). I would challenge companies that were misleading and harming people. I would issue call-to-actions to my listeners as to which elected officials needed to be phone bombed in order to change policy.

The 'aha moment' for me came when I was sitting with Senator Lindsey Graham (R-SC) prepared to hand him a $2,000 check from the Realtor's political action committee (RPAC). While there was never a written-agreement, there was an understanding about those sorts of meetings. We would give a campaign donation and he would take a listen to some of our issues. I was with several other Realtors at this meeting.

I was thoroughly impressed by how Senator Graham came to the meeting prepared to answer every question we had to ask of him. Clearly, his staff had done a fabulous job of prepping him. Most of my colleagues, in attendance, seemed nervous and unwilling to say much. Most Realtors are this way. A seemingly 'know everything if there's a commission involved,' but the minute they have to do anything that might make a difference they're paralyzed by incompetence or fear. I did most of the talking.

 What I realized is that our very rich industry was sitting in the room advising a top, elected official as to what policies we needed passed to line our pockets. Obviously, we framed it as what was best for the public (yeah right). It was what was best for our bank account. When several Realtors' Association's hand a sitting senator a check for $2,000 and cite the same issues demanding action, guess what happens? Action happens!

 This event left a lasting impression on me. There would be others of similar nature that would follow with elected officials.

 I stayed involved on the Board of Realtors as a director for a few months following this meeting. At the time, we were working on an initiative called 'raise the bar.' This was an effort to demand higher educational standards of all Realtors and ultimately (according to the mission statement) raise the barrier of entry to getting a license and becoming a member.

Oddly, our actions were anything but 'raise the bar.' I sat in multiple meetings where we were unwilling to demand much higher educational standards in order to maintain Realtor membership. We seemed, at best, tepid about working with state legislators to increase the number of hours required to obtain a licensee. At the time, you could sit in a classroom for eight straight days, take a test and have a license to work on almost all aspects of a $500,000 or even $5 million property. To me this was the financial equivalent of being able to obtain a medical license after a couple years of college.

I kept fighting what I would call the "Realtors' establishment" (long standing entitled employees and member-directors) only to no avail. It became obvious that raising the bar was a euphemism for helping average and below average people compete with exceptional people by giving the former an unfair advantage to take from the latter. I resigned.

I became the biggest critic of my own industry immediately. I began to admit to my audience that their beliefs about our industry were not only accurate but probably underestimated. I agreed that American consumers have every right to categorize Realtors in the same reputation category as shady used car salesman. Almost immediately, I began to see my own version of a Trump-like backlash.

Proud establishment members of the Realtors' community would call me unethical, unprofessional, and frequently a loose-cannon. Many of my comments and discussion sounded like Trump-outbursts. I would tell the stories of giving money in order to present policy issues and how disgusting I thought it was. I would admit that I was sitting there thinking the average person doesn't have the capacity to do this because they can't afford a $2,000 donation to their senator. The Realtor community was even more outraged at how unethical I was for telling insider secrets.

By the way, call up your senator and ask for a 20-minute sit-down meeting next week and see how that goes. Unless you have a donation you probably won't even receive a returned phone call.

Oddly, I was rewarded with more business than I could handle from turning from insider to whistle-blower. The 'industry,' the 'establishment,' or the status quo doesn't like it when an insider decides to be an outsider and tell the truth about what they observed inside. The labels and assaults I endured become an overwhelming example of classic psychological projection by Realtors projecting their harmful traits onto me.

I believe that the presidential campaign in 2016 unfolded with candidate Trump because he was tired of watching losers take advantage of American workers and businesses. He had been on the inside of all of these political circles. He had been friends with Democrats and Republicans alike. He was deeply rooted in the federal government bureaucracy and understood how it worked in terms of gaining approvals and working with the EPA and the transportation department. He knew all the secret rules of society just like I knew all the secret rules of the Realtors' society.

Here is what he and I share in common: We were both disgusted by the fact that we had to play the silly games in order to conduct business that simply makes sense. We were equally as bothered by the fact that success was becoming more about who you know and how well you could manipulate them than how great your idea was.

Trump has always been a bold-ideas guy. From the moment he entered Manhattan real estate, he looked like a failure waiting to happen in everyone's eyes but his own. He proved them all wrong. His presidential run was no different.

 By comparison, I always loved coming up with new ideas to attract customers and clients and help them get wealthy and buy real estate. As I stated before, I loved helping them make tough decisions that most people would deem folly. In turn, I helped many of them generate wealth. I understood that if I stayed true to that cause, my compensation would always be more than enough.

 I believe Trump operated with a similar style. His was different in that he provided value to properties that no one could see otherwise. It may be a different cause-and-effect but it operates on the same personal spirit of purpose before money.

 I know this tenet is true because I've had moments where money was my driving factor. I wouldn't realize it until the moment had passed and usually I was dealt a devastating blow or loss as a result. When money becomes the driving factor, failure becomes inevitable because you miss what's most important in the process.

 People are most important. We live in a country of industries and government who have reordered the importance by putting the process over the people. Everything in this chapter is a description of how we've morphed into a 'process over people' culture.

 I want to make one more point to drive this home. Process is not just the rules and procedures, it's also the institutions. Examples of institutions would include the National Association of Realtors, the Federal Bureau of Investigation, or the Internal Revenue Service. Over the years, each organization has experienced criminal activities and associates. These bad actors make conditions worse for everyone involved.

 Every time a bad actor figures out a way to circumvent the spirit of the rules and regulations of the group or agency, the reaction is more rules and regulations. In other words, we continue to build a roadmap for how illicit and illegal people can cheat the system by giving them a set of what they 'cannot do.' We set standards like 'raise the bar' but we never looked toward ethics and morality as a guide of how to do so. We always look for more rules and policies that make the struggle even greater for law-abiding associates and citizens. We're punitive in our approach harming only the good people and arming the bad people with a roadmap to deceit.

As a result, we **believe** we've cured a problem, but whistleblowing becomes even more complicated. I say all this to make the simple point that we recently learned the FBI had senior officials engaged in a plot to frame President Trump for collusion with the Russian government during the 2016 election. Since they were unsuccessful, they further engaged in a plot of abuse and illegal leaking of government intelligence in an attempt to damage Trump and ultimately serve as a catalyst for his impeachment.

It's likely that a host of uninvolved, senior FBI officials observed these atrocities, but said nothing. While I think they are just as complicit for being idle and apathetic in the event of frauds and conspiracy, there is a simple reason they didn't act: 'process over people.' The process is not just the rules and procedures but it's also the institution or organization.

In this FBI example, uninvolved officials who took no action were protecting their institution from embarrassment and a public relations nightmare instead of protecting the integrity of its mission for the people and country. When a culture becomes more interested in putting the process of its government and institutions as more important than the people, it begins to fail.

The irony of this illicit, immoral, and illegal behavior being perpetrated against Trump is ironic. I truly believe Trump sees his purpose as disrupting a culture that penalizes success, promotes entitlement, puts process over people, and removes accountability of government from the hands of the American people. That's why he ran for president.

Given that, there's no wonder that people in that corrupt system and believe in its superiority would want to think Trump really didn't want to win. After all, he ran for reasons that mean those disbelievers are the problem.

It is rare that successful people can become resentful of the conditions that enable their success. But, it is possible. I can say with certain clarity that I despise the conditions that exist in the real estate industry that afforded me an unbelievable amount of success and lifestyle. I would've rather just been the best, most experienced professional and never had to play the political games and deal with the resulting fallout from competitive losers in the industry. Such a condition simply doesn't exist, and it never will.

The reason I'm now in radio and media is because I feel that I can make a difference in my community by helping people understand why certain things are happening around them or to them. I've seen both sides of it, unlike most of my colleagues in the industry.

Make no mistake. Whether you like President Trump or not he ran for president to become president. He ran for president not to expose his company and his brand to the type of ridicule and criticism he's faced, but to make a difference and to 'right the wrongs' he experienced whether to his detriment or benefit. He could have continued building skyscrapers and expanded his company even more. By running for president, he reached for a legacy of doing something much bigger than himself.

When he says he ran for the forgotten people of America, trust me when I say this has weighed on him for decades while he has profited immensely. This was his moment of action.

In some ways, you have to become as powerful as the system in order to ever have a chance to change it. This means you have to profit from the legal-wrongs of a society in order to garner the tools and resources to fight against it.

I didn't say you have to cheat people to gain the power to fix the system. I said you have to first become successful while being moral and ethical inside a corrupt system before you can become powerful enough to change it.

Trump ran to win and fix the incompetence that he was forced to experience for the last four decades.

CHAPTER EIGHTEEN
Dealing with the Naysayers

At every step of your career and life, there are going to be naysayers.

Some of them are going to be your closest friends and family who are simply afraid that your success or path may leave them behind. While this may sound selfish, it may not be. It may simply be that some of your friends and family see your potential and realize that, at some point, your relationship may no longer be mutually beneficial and they will be the one dragging you down.

Each relationship we encounter throughout our life has a purpose. Some friends are there for a season to help us move from one phase of our life to another. Some are lifelong friends. Most are not ever at the same economic or professional skill level.

One of my best friends is a real estate agent that I met in 2003. He was a couple of years younger than me and had just graduated from college. I was already successful making several hundred thousand dollars per year in real estate sales. We had begun recruiting real estate agents to help us with all of the leads our company was producing.

On paper, my friend had all of the assets and talents to be an agent. But, when I met him, my gut instinct told me he had no chance of success in this industry.

 First, he was a tightwad. So, instead of telling him candidly what I thought, I just gave him a proven plan for success in real estate. I told him to quit his job, sell his old car, buy something fitting for real estate sales, and immediately begin investing in his image. We looked at the amount of money he would have to live and determined he could make it six months without any income before he would be out of money. I had no doubt he would reject this plan and move on. After all, he was too big of a tightwad and I was not yet as candid with people as I am now.
 Instead, he did exactly what I told him to do and two years later was making nearly $300,000 a year. In this case, I was the naysayer, but fortunately I didn't say anything. He was one of the most difficult mentees of the dozens I've coached over the years. He asked lots of questions, overthought every decision, and needed help with every aspect of the real estate transaction for the first two years. While his sales did bring profit to the company, it was grossly out of proportion with almost every other real estate

agent because of the amount of work and support he required.

He and I both met our wives virtually the same week, and he flew across the country to attend my small wedding in Las Vegas. We've been on dozens of trips together including destinations, boating excursions, and cruises. I've said everything that I've written in this book to his face, so I have no doubt he's laughing as he's reading what I've just wrote.

After a few years, I faced three incredible challenges. The first was the necessity of buying out my business partner in what became a bombshell event for our real estate company. In anticipation of my lawsuit against my business partner, I told this friend what was about to happen. I didn't ask him to get involved since he still worked for the company. However, I ask him to be on the lookout for odd behavior that could be damaging to the company for the week I took a hiatus to prepare my lawsuit. I believed I could trust him and he didn't let me down.

The next crisis was the financial calamity I faced during the great recession. He watched me lose millions of dollars in a single year as real estate values and sales collapsed. Many of my friendships and associations changed during that time. Our friendship got stronger.

Next, came my near divorce. As usual in divorces, both my wife and I drew a line in the sand looking for allies and enemies. He refused. While he supported me in many ways, he never engaged in any of the toxic bashing, accusations, or diatribes. Instead he found a way to remain friends with both of us and ultimately support our happiness in the end. We learned during this time that taking sides on a friend's divorce is almost a sure pathway to end that friendship.

What I've described here is a friend not for a season but for a lifetime. You never know until nearly two decades have passed. Our friendship has developed into one where we can sincerely trust each other's advice as dependable, selfless, and in the spirit of each other's success.

I'm blessed to have another friend I met in college who has mutually experienced many of life's challenges but from a different vantage point. Oddly, this friend is liberal while I'm conservative. This has created an interesting debate at times.

We agree on almost everything while disagreeing on how to accomplish it. Our debates are sometimes aggressive, loud, and scary to people who don't know us very well. We've probably helped each other grow in terms of our thinking, in ways we can never imagine because we've been debating life and politics for nearly three decades without ever allowing the discourse to become personal.

He's like the older brother I never had and definitely a lifelong friend. Every time we see each other whether it's been a week or nearly a year, we pick up right where we left off.

These friends have never been naysayers with what I 'stand for' or who I am. This is not to say they don't question me at times, but they never tell me what I can't do or shouldn't. They always encourage me.

I have other friends that I've known for a few years that I believe may become as close as the two I've outlined above. However, I've learned that only time can prove whether a friendship is for a season or a lifetime.

I'll later discuss more about how to maintain relationships that are lasting with people with which you have many disagreements by changing your tone from change maker to listener. This valuable detail will appear in chapter 24, "Curiosity."

I have had other friendships during seasons of my life where it was a different experience. At times I would be told that an idea was ridiculous. Certain friends have questioned my success by asking "when is enough, enough?" At times, I've had friends that constantly reminded me of my weaknesses as a way to control me. Sadly, we often allow these people to remain in our lives for far too long.

Most of the time, they are simply afraid that our success may leave them behind. At times their demeaning commentary is an attempt to control us in order to focus on themselves or what they want. In other instances, they simply treated our friendship as a competition.

The bottom line is that you have to get rid of naysayers in your life. You should only surround yourself with people who challenge your thinking and support your decisions. To be clear, I'm not saying you should seek friends who approve of behavior that is damaging to you such as hard drugs, alcohol abuse, or other illicit circumstances. I'm simply saying that when you feel abused by a certain friend or relative on a frequent basis, you probably are correct.

There is a form of Stockholm syndrome that we develop with friends who constantly question our integrity, intent, or reasoning behind actions we take in our lives. If this keeps happening, you have to ask yourself why this person would want to be friends with someone like you. You should not be 'a project' to a relative or friend. You should never feel negated by a friend or relative. While instances of this are acceptable, consistencies of it are not.

Once you rid your life of naysayers, expect them to become vocal critics of you.
Many of the people who've been fired or rejected by Trump are now the people the media loves to parade as "insiders telling the story about what kind of guy he really is." Oddly, in our modern day 'fakestream media,' they fail to describe the circumstances for which this newfound critic was ousted from their relationship or employment.

Inconvenient details that undermine the agenda of the media are frequently never revealed unless you dig deeper.

If someone is found to have worked for Trump and has something negative to say about him, we can't spoil the moment with inconvenient little facts like they were fired for stealing.

Just remember, when someone claims to have had prior access close to Trump and has something negative to say, they may have been a naysayer, creating a toxic environment that led to hearing the famous words of Donald J. Trump: "you're fired!"

The point here is that Trump is the 45th president of the United States. He has enemies resulting from his own mistakes and from the mistakes of others who he held accountable. He has many more than the average American because, in order to attain his level of success, you have to get damn good at getting the naysayers out of your way.

Start reflecting on who in your life is holding you down, TODAY. Make today the beginning of the most successful phase of your life by getting rid of negative naysayers and abusers who will drain you of success and passion otherwise.

CHAPTER NINETEEN
A Nagging Dream or Desire

President Trump has been talking about running for president since the late 1980s. He always said that if he ever ran he thought he could win. He also said that he would only run if he thought the country had an absence of leadership and that he could make a real difference.

This history of commentary got omitted from the political discourse during the 2016 election as many people thought he was running for the prestige or the marketing effect it would create for the Trump brand in his company.

Being president was likely a deeply-rooted, nagging desire of Trump from the moment it was first suggested in the 1980s. Let me tell you how to recognize and develop these nagging desires.

After the election of 2012, it was my belief that this country had lost its way. It had reelected a man with virtually no leadership skills and inept management skills who had also surrounded himself with a host of bad actors with political agendas that were incredibly damaging to our country.

I was demoralized and disgusted that the American electorate had become so inept as to not recognize how much damage was being done to our great nation. This was less about President Obama individually, as our 44th president, and more about the policies coming from his White House.

I've always maintained that President Obama appears to me to be a great husband and a wonderful father with strong convictions about what he desires in terms of agenda. In fact, I think he could have been a much better president if he had waited until he was 55 or 60 to run for office. He simply wasn't experienced enough to be managing 2 million federal employees and a $4 trillion budget. As a result, he attracted people who ultimately were able to convince him they supported his policies while simultaneously working on their own competing agendas. Lacking experience, leadership skills, and effective management skills he was unable to police his own executive branch. As a result our country was spiraling culturally and politically.

Meanwhile, I was experiencing a transformation of a great industry: the real estate industry. It was becoming demoralizing, brutal, full of red tape, and nearly impossible. At the same time, I had fully recovered from the crash and was making more money than ever before. Smart people can perform even better in these circumstances because they can find solutions to problems that government or market related chaos creates. That's what I did.

Around this time, I finally realized for the first time that I had never gotten out of radio. It was in 2012 and 2013 that I realized that I have simply continued my radio career and monetized it through real estate. The last two years I had been doing fill-in work for the morning show of our local talk radio station while continuing my weekend housing show. I had developed a strong set of political opinions. I have found that my strong political opinions injected into my real estate show actually were endearing me to the audience of customers and clients even more.

I want you to notice here that I didn't just start being political. I had gone through a series of successes and failures in my life where government had played a positive and negative role. I had operated a company with lawyers on retainer and hundreds of employees and was doing business in multiple states. My political opinions were based upon experience of the effects of politics on business and success.

Therefore, I had developed a secret weapon that I wasn't yet able to understand just how valuable it was. I didn't just have an opinion on how politics and government impact business and individual success; I was something of an accidental expert in it.

In 2013, the very successful morning show host on our radio station resigned after his wife tragically died of cancer. A burning and 'nagging' desire arose at that moment. I had filled in for him several times during his wife's cancer treatment. I felt compelled to apply for the position. I was rather confident I could get it. However, doing a four hour morning show on talk radio is a full time job if there ever was one.

It's not just four hours on the radio. It's also about one to two hours of prep work for every hour you are live on the station. Then there's meetings with advertisers, the typical corporate 'meetings about meetings,' and community appearances to promote your show. I had far too many clients depending on me to 'kick them to the curb' and take over the show. The income was also a pittance compared to what I was already earning in real estate.

Disclaimer: While I had transformed to being less focused on money, taking a job that was full time for roughly 20% of my current income would be more akin to suicide than evolution and purpose.

The opportunity passed by for those reasons, but my desire didn't. I started doing a morning commentary that was supposed to be two or three minutes each weekday morning at the highest point of listenership each day. This was so successful for my business that after a couple of months, I had my highest month ever of sales. My two staff and I closed or wrote approximately $15 million of business in just one month. We had very profitable months before I sold my company, with smaller sales than that (from 200-400 agents).

Having toyed with the idea of doing that morning show, I now had a problem. Real estate had become 'a job.' Most of my time was riddled with paperwork, crisis management, and understanding new regulations that posed an existential threat to our business model.

'Dodd-Frank' was a bill passed and signed by President Obama that was supposed to thwart future financial crises such as the one that occurred in 2008-2011. Instead, it made life hell for the real estate industry and the people it served (re: YOU). Clients were getting upset because we could no longer do simple things that used to make sense. Moreover, every deal became more expensive, making it nearly impossible to give the kind of personalized service that my clients expected.

Thanks to leftists ideas and 'feelings,' gone were the days where smart industry insiders and their clients could make wise, mutual decisions. Now, we gave all of those decisions over to a set of rules that every institution must follow regardless of whether they made sense or not. It would be things like the free refrigerator. Even if I were offering it to the buyer in the home sale, it wouldn't be allowed to be in the contract. So, we faced a real situation of offering something that is common in real estate transactions but finding it literally illegal to put the deal in writing. This meant the government created a host of egregious, unintentional consequences that meant we had to trust the seller would actually do what they said they would do. If we attempted to create a written agreement, it was literally considered mortgage fraud. If we put it in the contract and disclosed it, the buyer's loan would be denied.

I think you can agree that what I just described is simply idiotic. I was becoming very frustrated with being yelled at by people over issues I had literally zero control to change.

After a few months, I attempted to convince the talk radio station to carve out an afternoon slot for a local show. I was bluntly told that programming decisions were made by the corporate bosses in the 'ivory tower' and there was no way they would allow it. During this time, a very popular local talk host moved to a new radio station working for a local owner. I contacted the owner and pitched the same idea. He gave me the morning show.

During this time, I was able to cover the many infractions of incumbent Governor Nikki Haley (R-SC), the demise of the most powerful politician in the state of South Carolina, State Speaker of The House Bobby Harrell(R-SC), and many local public policy issues that were damaging to the community.

In one instance, I outed a local political action committee that was attempting to stop a real estate development by forging a series of lies about the development and its developers. When I uncovered and revealed that the leader of this 'action group' worked for the firm who did initial design for the project, I exposed him as a hypocrite. He was fired and sued me. He later became a City Councilman and the case never went to trial.

After a couple of years, I realized that my efforts were becoming a challenge (in terms of media) because I was on a small AM station in a medium sized market.

Realizing that I had to be in an arena that didn't have such a low ceiling, I moved to Atlanta, the 8th largest media market in the nation. Shortly after the move, I hosted two radio shows on Salem Media Group's local outlets and had dozens of articles published in national outlets, reaching tens of millions of people while also becoming a contributor to major international television networks and radio outlets.

The point of telling you this is to understand that sometimes you have to make bold moves, recognize your weaknesses, and step far outside of your comfort zone. Just when starting over seemed like the opposite of what to do, that's exactly what I did.

The point is that we all have a burning desire inside of us to do something for a specific reason that only we can individually understand. Mine is a simple agenda: to find the truth behind the stories that are changing our culture and expose it to as many people as I possibly can. I want our country to remain great and it takes an army of us doing what I've just described to insure that happens.

I'm not interested in stroking my ego by gaining popularity. I'd be just as happy not being a public figure and living on a farm. However, we are not put on this earth to idle through life. Sometimes doing what you love comes with a high price and sometimes it produces unimaginable financial and personal success. I'll leave that part of my destiny up to God.

The point of sharing these two stories is to help you find your nagging desire. Without question President Trump has had a nagging desire to run for president for decades. It is without question that I had a nagging desire to be a media analyst and radio host for years. I wish I had done it sooner.

I hope you will identify your nagging desire and act upon it sooner than later.

Figuring out what your nagging desire is, (sometimes called purpose) is not always easy. However, once you find it, it becomes the easiest process known to man. You will find that the pathway toward your purpose or nagging desire is almost always laid in advance. The process isn't easy. However, when you are on the 'right track' you'll find doors opening up for you that you never saw or expected. That's the only explanation of why I almost immediately landed a radio gig and national contributor status shortly thereafter when I moved to Atlanta.

I started in radio and media when I was 16 years old. I was making a multiple, six figure income by my mid-20s. I owned a company with over 400 people and employees by the time I was 30. I was worth millions of dollars and lost most of it by my early 30s. I earned a lot of it back by my late 30s with the help of my very intelligent and successful wife. I found my true friends and relationships. People who I'd helped the most early in their career, were now helping me in unimaginable ways I could have never predicted.

I have lost millions of dollars. My reputation was damaged because of that. I nearly got divorced at one point. During the financial calamity I lost a number of friends who were no longer interested in the 'poorer version' of me. I could have retired (at the age of 30) in 2007, but by 2009 I had to work to earn it all back.

What did all this mean? It took me a couple of years, mentally reliving the negative experiences to understand that this burning desire that didn't really make financial sense made all the sense in the world. I would be one of the few people in media who had experience with politics, business, journalism, and culture. This is why I successfully predicted the electoral outcome of the presidential election of 2016 months before it happened.

My financial calamity and the process of working through it taught me the incredible skill of how to negotiate with banks to conduct short sales for myself. When you own three dozen properties mostly leveraged by mortgages, I need not tell you how much of a crash course I was given. By the time most people were facing the worst of the financial fallout, I was rebuilding my balance sheet. I was able to empathize with the emotions and fears of people as they experienced sleepless nights, worried about their financial condition and their home. In many cases, I was able to tell people how to save their home and how to avoid foreclosure. I was serving people by assisting them in selling a home, while saving their credit and preventing bankruptcy. It was extremely rewarding.

Those five years of substantial and unimaginable income, while the rest of the country suffered deeply, gave me the foundation to be able to take the risk to pursue my burning desire of returning to media/radio and exposing the truth. This book is just another extension of that. My goal in this book is to help you see a different side of the ascension of President Trump to the White House and additionally help you tap into those elements within you that you may not know exist.

To that point, you may have a burning desire in you that you keep ignoring that may represent your overall purpose in life. It may seem unaffordable and the naysayers in your life may tell you it's crazy to pursue it. Don't listen to them!

Instead, listen to your heart. Talk with your spouse. Find a friend who is almost always supportive but unafraid to challenge you. Listen to what they say and drown out the noise of naysayers. Be willing to make sacrifices, financially, in order to feel more rewarded about how you spend your life.

Don't be surprised when you find yourself making more money doing what you love than doing what you have to do to make money. Don't focus on the money. Be aware of it. Focus on what you feel called to do and what excites you in your career. You'll do a much better job of what you love than "what you have to do to survive."

You may think that this is the point that you should lay down the book and get to work on your purpose. Wrong! If you miss the next couple chapters, you'll miss some of the most critical facts about how naysayers will attempt to stop you in your tracks.

CHAPTER TWENTY
Refusing to Follow the Rules and Getting Away With It

Okay! Just to be clear, this chapter has nothing to do with breaking the laws, being unethical, or being immoral.

This chapter is about breaking arbitrary, unilateral rules that curtail your success usually created by people who have nothing in mind but controlling you. The name of this book is the "Trump in You" so let's start with a classic Trump example.

Most politicians follow a set of rules, talking points, and policy papers and they rarely answer questions outside of the scope of those robotic standards. That's 'the rule' of politics. Trump didn't follow any of that; he broke all those rules. Unwritten, unilateral rules of society, government, or industry are in place to control the masses and support the status quo. If you want to make change, you're not going to do so by following those ridiculous and usually harmful rules.

Trump said whatever he felt, whenever he wanted, and answered almost every question whether it was popular to do so or not throughout the 2016 campaign.

There has always been a standing rule in the real estate industry that you don't speak negatively of the National Association of Realtors or its local organizations. This rule is drawn from the Realtors' code of ethics which specifically states that you don't demean or disparage other Realtors in order to obtain business. After my resignation as a member-director from the Board of Realtors, I had a clear understanding of the 'black and white' nature of these rules.

These rules were in place to keep me from arbitrarily calling another Realtor unethical or disparaging him/her as a person. I agree with that particular written rule and its spirit.

However, a large amount of ignorance pollutes the real estate industry. The rules became unilateral and unwritten in our industry which caused most of my competitors to believe it unethical even to compare stats against other competitors in order to obtain a listing or client. I broke the rules! I would tell potential clients things such as "the other agent you are interviewing has only sold four homes in the last 16 months." Many of my competitors would become outraged. Why is a black and white statistic unethical? I'm simply selling the value proposition of my experience versus my competitor. I do realize that by doing this I'm giving myself an advantage and presenting a disadvantage to my competitor. There's a word for this. It's called "sales." If you don't like it, get a real job and don't get into sales!!!

I didn't give a damn what anybody thought because there was no rule of ethics or legality I was breaking. I was simply breaking the unspoken rules that allowed inexperienced agents to hide from their inexperience and cause damage to members of the public by deluding them into thinking they could do as good of a job as someone with my experience and track record. Sadly, the National Association of Realtors promotes this insane behavior so they can increase the number of paying members on their roster.

There was also no written rule that said I couldn't be critical of the National Association of Realtors. However, when I did, there was immediate and extensive backlash. Sometimes, the backlash I received actually did break the code of ethics, but since they were defending the institution (process over people), there would never be a penalty. When these attacks occurred, instead of being beaten into submission as most people would, I'd double down. After a while, people realized that their attempts to silence me would have the opposite of the intended effect. I would actually respond to their attempt to silence me by being even stronger with my opinion.

Do you see the parallel between this business example and Trump running for the presidency? Every time he said something that was against the unwritten rules of politics, and the media and his competitors went nuts, he responded with even more of what made them nutty. Who are they to tell him what he can and can't say when he's running for President of the United States?

Almost no one would ever say I was incompetent or ineffective in serving my clients. They would call me unethical. I was amazed at the number of clients who would tell me, as they were signing a listing agreement with my company, what other people would say about me - which directly broke the **real** and written rules. It was rewarding to have my new clients tell me that they appreciated the fact that another agent was literally calling me unethical for standing up for consumer rights.

Let me put it another way. I was playing the idiotic real estate industry for the fools they are. I was allowing them to think they might have a chance to control me while proving to people I was more qualified and capable. As my competitors became so focused on me, they validated me.

I saw Trump do this repeatedly during the 2016 presidential election. Knowing the unspoken, unilateral, and ridiculous rules of politics he would bait his opponents into reacting with outrage at his so-called bad behavior only to break them in a calculating fashion.

Listen! When people operate based on unwritten and unspoken standards as though they are real rules or laws, they are setting themselves up for failure. It's lazy and apathetic to assume you should always do what your industry or organization has always done. You are only required to do what is ethical, legal, and moral.

Moreover, when you allow your competition to frame the debate, choose the topic, and predetermine the right and wrong answer, you will always lose that game. Never allow your competitors to bait you into playing their game. Bait them into playing yours by rejecting their arbitrary rules and procedures that have no bearing on ethics, legality, or morality.

Some could argue that Trump's actions during the elections were immoral. I can buy that argument while at the same time asserting that many of his opponents were even worse. Who are we to judge morality? I don't believe I'm morally superior to any other person, so I choose not to judge morals in the context of words. Almost all of the outrage against Trump was a reaction to his words. Instead, I looked strictly at his business record and behavior and found a lot of positive attributes that said to me that he appeared to be mostly a smart and ethical businessman.

You may disagree with my last sentence. If you choose to judge Trump's business record solely on all the things he did wrong or his limited number of failures instead of his successes and accomplishments, that's your prerogative. You'll lose in life with such an approach, but so be it.

The reason Trump received such an insane volume of outrage is because most people operate with a sheep mentality. Moreover, the media distorts the true sentiment and beliefs of actual American voters. Sheep follow the herd the same way each day expecting the same result each time. Unfortunately, there comes the day where the herd leads them to slaughter. At that point, it's too late.

Successful people never allow themselves to be herded.

You will struggle to find success and never reach your potential as long as you follow the arbitrary and unilateral rules of your industry, community, or society.

Unspoken rules are behavioral constraints imposed in organizations or society that are not voiced or written down and are intended to contain or limit you. Society depends on people like you to remain stuck in your career and perform the low to mid-level jobs. People like you are necessary for society to function. Most people will never realize why they are stuck in the middle. Therefore, you don't have to remain there.

I'm simply telling you that you don't have to be stuck in the middle. When everyone follows these rules, an elite few are empowered as arbitrary enforcers.

An apolitical example of arbitrary rules of society is tipping at a restaurant or for other service. Tipping is an unwritten rule that I find disgusting. If I receive exceptional service, I give an exceptional tip. If I receive unacceptable service, I give no tip. Apparently, this isn't fair to the service industry. I don't care. I don't believe in rewarding apathetic and incompetent behavior. I'd rather save my hard earned money to give to the few people who really earned it than to continue being another one of the sheep enabling incompetent service providers to believe they are providing acceptable service.

Another problem I have is voicemail. Unless my client leaves me a voicemail, I am not obligated to return it. Voicemail controls me if I allow it. I would prefer to receive an email with the pertinent details for which I need to respond, so that I can read it in one minute and respond - while ridding myself of yet another unwanted task. Society's unwritten rules tell us that if you receive a phone call you should return the call. Not me! I respond with an email. Doing so communicates an appropriate answer and doesn't allow someone else to control my time.

Most of the calls I receive are unsolicited, not from family, and certainly not from clients to whom I owe a fiduciary responsibility. I owe my family, friends, and clients my time - no one else.

For most of my life I've heard the phrase "respect authority." Many times I have found 'authority' to be entitled, incompetent, and destructive. I refuse to respect anyone who is incompetent and destructive in their behavior. I don't care what title they have or their role; I give my respect to those who earn it. A title is worthless.

I prefer serving in leadership positions where I have direct access to the top decision makers, without being given a title myself. This eliminates the need for certain people to feel the need to kiss my ass and for others to dislike me for the perceived power I have over them. Real power is being an influential player in your company or organization without being popularly known for the role you play.

After years of experience being a parent of school age children, I've noticed an interesting phenomenon in that other parents seem tepid when it comes to challenging the 'authority' at school. Reflecting on this, it seems that many parents are afraid that if they challenge administrators and teachers that their children will be penalized in terms of grades or beneficial program access.

The school system, in general, has created this impression. The fact that parents allow it to exist is stunning to me. If I don't like something that's happening at my children's school, I aggressively speak against it without concern for how they may react. If my children don't get to be part of the latest 'group' created by the school, good!

I also dislike people who put those bumper stickers on their car that say, "my child is an honor student at 'xyz' school." Who cares? Those sort of stupid, idiotic bumper stickers say to society that "my child is good because of their grades." I would much rather be the parent of a 'straight C student' that learns how to defend him or herself, treats others with respect, and promotes good values in society than some selfish brat with a 4.0 GPA that no one likes. Society defines 'good' as being a series of scores that don't reflect ethics, morals, or behaviors. However, the minute a child or adult does something transformative that threatens the people who feel entitled to everything, they are suddenly 'unethical.'

Here's what our public school system and 'my child' bumper stickers really say to our children: "Just make straight A's, don't break any of our arbitrary rules, act nice when you're being watched, and you'll be considered good. We don't care how you act when it doesn't matter or we're not measuring you."

 At times, I've been asked to be "more professional" in my communication. My response is always that "when you properly address the issue at hand, I will have no reason to be unprofessional." This is another example of people saying that so long as you comply with us, you're good. If it doesn't bother us (no matter how wrong it is), it doesn't matter. Haven't you noticed our society is progressively becoming a bunch of people who put on a show in public and act the exact opposite in private? These examples explain why!

 Finally, one of my business pet peeves, especially in the wake of the financial crisis, is signing documents in order to purchase a car, a piece of equipment, or buy a house. We recently paid cash for a car and planned to have it shipped across the country. On the day our trucker was to pick up the car, we were informed that we didn't sign the documents correctly for our limited liability company (the legal purchaser). The 'bean-counter' in the back office at the dealership wanted us to include the name of the LLC in our signature line. It wasn't acceptable to simply sign "Bryan Crabtree, as president." They wanted my signature to read, "Bryan Crabtree as president for XYZ, LLC."

This is beyond an ignorant request by the 'bean-counter.' It's just plain stupid. The LLC already is listed on the contract and purchase agreement. By signing the contract, I only have to look at the top of the contract to see that my signature is on behalf of the LLC. It already says that. By forcing me to change my own unique and personal signature, they're actually making the potential confusion more likely.

This ridiculous signature issue meant we had to cancel the shipping arrangement which likely would've cost us a fee and start the process again. Then we would've had to wait for new documents to arrive and delay the shipment of the car for a few days. I refused this unwritten rule of society and told him that I was offended by their assertion that I did not sign properly for my own limited liability company.

I informed them that they "had received our funds and our documents two days prior and that if the car was not on the truck today there would be hell to pay." I refuse to let back office, bean-counters tell me how to operate my business and sign contracts on its behalf. If they want my business, they'll earn it by doing it my way or I'll go somewhere else.

Our president is no different. Most people are sheep. They do what they're told by the people and companies for which they do business. This condition is so bad that when someone like me actually has the nerve to hold them accountable for abusing consumers and their time, they are beyond offended. These people do not have my best interests at heart.

Some people would say "what's wrong with just signing the documents again?" I would reply, "everything." It's my signature and no one is going to tell me how to sign my name, especially when I'm not getting a loan and I'm the one paying cash for the car. Why should I pay a shipping penalty and wait for more documents to be sent (again) because someone wants something that they think is necessary but isn't.

Stop trying to be liked by the people for which you do business. Instead, take care of your own business and force them to earn the right to have your business.

Many people dislike Trump because he cannot be controlled. He does not allow others to tell him arbitrarily how to behave, achieve his goals, or facilitate his endeavors. Given his lack of any criminal record, it is safe to say he follows the laws while breaking the unwritten and arbitrary rules of society. As a result, he has created one of the most successful real estate companies in the world and became the 45th president of the United States.

 Find the "Trump in You" by no longer following unwritten rules. Reject them. Make people play your game - not theirs. This is not an easy thing to do, because sometimes you have to become a version of yourself that you won't like very much. You'll have to be strong, candid, and at times extremely demanding in order to fight for your values and to protect yourself from being abused by businesses and other people.

 In my car shipping scenario I described, I wasn't nice. I told the salesperson that I was 'pissed' and I found this typical of purchasing their brand of vehicle. I said to him everything I've said in this chapter about those situations and more. Regretfully, it takes this aggressive and sometimes egregious approach in order to keep others from abusing you. Within minutes of that phone call, the car was put on the carrier and the problem was resolved.

 My pressure caused the 'bean-counter' to go to their boss who had the authority to make the situation disappear. Sometimes these 'bean-counters' just love the control they have over other people and sometimes they are just doing their job for people who rarely have to face the consequences of the stupid rules they arbitrarily create.

Had I not 'lost it' on the telephone, the process would've gone on for several more days and I'm certain that something else would've been wrong with the paperwork. I have no patience for back-office 'bean-counters' who get high on making the rest of us fill out more forms and waste more of our time with their redundant processes, because they don't have control over anyone or anything else in their lives. You may think this is a minor issue but if you want to be successful in life you have to take control of these issues or they will collectively overwhelm you and steal your productivity and purpose.

The next time you watch a political analyst on one of the cable news outlets bashing Trump, just remember the individual has likely never signed a payroll check, taken out a business loan to expand their company, or dealt with a contractor who didn't complete his job. Accordingly, it's easy for them to judge someone else's style or behavior as unprofessional, unpresidential, or egregious when they have never really accomplished anything in business other than their job of vomiting ignorance across America.

 Break the rules, disrupt your industry, and deny those who wish to control you the ability to do so.

CHAPTER TWENTY-ONE
Trump's Moments of Victory

I wanted to write a chapter reflecting on some of the most polarizing moments of the 2016 presidential election. These will be moments you remember, but may not fully understand in terms of how greatly they impacted the victory that made the 45th president of the United States Donald J. Trump.

The Escalator
When Trump rode down the Trump Tower escalator in May 2015 and announced his candidacy for president, the mainstream media and political class thought it was a big joke.

Moreover, they were outraged by the notion that Trump called some immigrants from Mexico "rapists and murderers." This was the beginning of Trump being called a "bigot and a racist."

Most people would be terrified to earn those stripes, but Trump wasn't. They were badges of honor. What the mainstream media and the political class perpetuate has become the antithesis of what the majority of the American people desire. While the media was consumed by overanalyzing and vomiting their opinion all over

America about how despicable Trump's comments were, the American people were cheering them.

 The American people generally knew that saying a large number of illegal immigrants were criminals, was not inaccurate. It may have been harsh to actually have a political candidate force us to face that tragic reality, but many people were thinking, "finally someone willing to say what I'm afraid to say…"

 While comments like "rapists and murders" seemed to be the kind that would end the candidacy of Trump, his lack of an apology upon the media's demand would actually serve to propel his campaign on. It put 'wind in his sails.' The 'rapists and murderers' comment was an extremely valuable foundation for his campaign, not because he said it, but because he doubled down on it when it seemed the unpopular thing to do.

'Small Hands'
 I remember sitting backstage in the press filing room while watching the Republican primary presidential debate as Trump responded to Sen. Marco Rubio's (R-FL) 'small hands' comment.

Rubio had made the following comment on the campaign trail: "He's taller than me, he's like 6'2", which is why I don't understand why his hands are the size of someone who is 5'2". Have you seen his hands?"

 Trump's debate response would be an innuendo about the size of his hands being no indication of the size of his manhood. He said "I can assure you there is no problem there." Many were stunned by such a comment in a presidential candidate. Others thought it was hilarious. This debate took the tone of an episode of 'Jerry Springer' on television. On one level it was an embarrassing display of just how divided we've become. By contrast, years of pent-up resentment was pouring into the national discourse giving us some hope of healing. Most people were embarrassed, I saw it as the 'rock bottom' that is necessary before most recoveries.

 Trump had effectively baited almost every candidate on stage into attempting to play his game of outrage politics. Rubio engaged in personal attacks as did most others. Their problem is that they were politicians not experienced in playing the game of a businessman. One by one, as they were baited into engaging in these personal attacks they began to show a side of themselves that none of us had seen. It was the exact opposite of what they had told us they were for years. It was a stark contrast with their well-crafted (and apparently fraudulent) images.

While many would call Trump's behavior, even style, childish and unbecoming of a president, it was expected of him having seen him on countless shows and documentaries over the years. We had not seen senators and former governors behave in the same way. As a result, many of them damaged their reputations, revealed a fraudulent, hidden, and petulant side and systematically ruined their chances of becoming president.

Trump wisely baited each one of them into behaving with his style and in his arena. None of them detected it before it was too late, including his eventual general election opponent, Democrat Hillary Clinton.

'Low Energy Jeb'

This one phrase alone may have single-handedly been responsible for destroying former Governor Jeb Bush's (R-FL) $100 million campaign war-chest and ultimately ending his campaign for president. From phrases like "Lying Ted," to "Crooked Hillary," to "Low Energy Jeb," Trump effectively branded his opponents with their weaknesses.

He made a mockery out of the fact that Bush had more than $100 million in campaign funding and still couldn't reach double digits in the polls. He properly and effectively tied this to how he would waste voters' tax money as president and be ineffective in serving their needs even with the resources of our government. As Bush fought back, he did so in a way that solidified the moniker of 'low energy.' Bush reacted by saying, "you can't insult your way to the presidency." That appeared to me as an admission that Trump was right and that Bush had no rebuttal other than to paint Trump as a bad guy. Regardless of how you view Trump and his antics, he convinced you that Bush was not what we needed as president.

It was as if though Trump was playing a game of 'presidential whack-a-mole.' As soon as one opponent was obliterated another one would rise up in the polling, seemingly the benefactor of the last victim's demise. Up next? Carly Fiorina.

Carly Fiorina: "Look at that Face"

While I thought this moment was low, even for candidate Trump, it was still highly effective.

There wasn't much wrong with Carly Fiorina as a candidate, except her style and according to Trump, but not me, her looks. She was a successful businesswoman who was a change-maker for women in the corporate hierarchy as she substantially grew Hewlett-Packard organically and through its merger with Compaq during her tenure as CEO. She had been a formidable candidate in California politics as a Republican – no small feat. She was deeply rooted in conservative causes as an influential politician and presented the kind of business acumen and leadership background our country desperately needed in this era.

For a fleeting moment, she was one of Trump's biggest threats. Even for Trump, articulating that a female president would struggle representing America on the world stage, was off-limits. One would have predicted that commenting on a female opponent's looks would have been as well.

Comments by Trump regarding her looks were as much a slam of Fiorina's style as they were her appearance. Her presentation seemed very preachy and almost nagging at times, even if her message was appealing. By commenting on her looks, Trump reminded the American people subtly that women are still disrespected by many countries that are both allies and foes. In other words, "she may struggle more in negotiations on behalf of America than a male president." He knew that was not a comment he could actually say out loud.

 My writing of these observations is in no way an endorsement of that belief. However, even many women in America admit that they still have a legitimate concern of how a female president may be received by other countries.

 I think this concern is invalid, but there are millions who think this way. Fiorina could have made a great leader. I have no doubt a female will become president of this great nation in my lifetime not because they are female, but because they are the most qualified candidate at the time.

Megyn Kelly's "Blood Coming out of Her Wherever"

 In the first Republican primary presidential debate, held by Fox News, it was obvious from the onset that Megyn Kelly, a Fox Anchor, was going to attempt to play a game of 'gotcha' with Trump. She attacked him, in the style of a question, about his treatment and language regarding women. In classic Trump style, he quipped back "only Rosie O'Donnell." The audience chuckled while Kelly attempted to regain control.

Trump and O'Donnell had a long and notorious public feud against each other, thus why he made that response.

There were a series of questions aimed at Trump that seemed less in the interest of getting policy details from him and more about proving he was unfit as president. This was Kelly's style. She's one of the main people that first helped me developed my 'be nice crowd' theory. I always thought she was nothing more than a beautiful woman playing a role that would garner her the most attention. I never saw her as someone who really believed the shit she was peddling. This debate and her questions proved that.

In response to the debate, Trump said that Kelly had 'blood coming out of her eyes and blood coming out of her wherever" referring to the style of her questions. He maintained that she was "out for blood." the media and the political class saw it differently. They thought Trump was referring to Kelly having her menstrual cycle. Obviously, no man in America ever comments about that, right?

I asked that snarky question because the media and the political class have created arbitrary rules that say politicians cannot act like real adult citizens. They must act "above that." Trump was the first one to shatter their rules and expose them as frauds.

This was a defining point in the Republican presidential primary. This was effectively the end of Kelly's tenure at Fox News. She would host her show there for many more months but a substantial portion of the audience despised her after her treatment of Trump. Many people believed that she was a fraud only interested in being part of the news instead of covering it.

In the end, Trump's 'blood' comment would expose Kelly as being disingenuous and fraudulent in the opinions and views she would produce and share. He would gain support in the wake of the comment, not lose any. Clearly, more people disagreed with the media and his opponents' characterization of it than agreed, or simply didn't care either way.

People who supported Trump would see this comment as simply being a comment about rage and not her menstrual cycle. People who would never support Trump saw it as an antifeminist comment revolving around her emotional instability during her menstrual cycle. Undecided voters would be generally unswayed by it except that it would leave a proverbial question mark over the head of Kelly regarding her integrity.

More bluntly, it made her irrelevant except to people who would never support Trump anyway. She had rendered herself useless, ineffective, and irrelevant to the election.

The Debate Boycott

As a result of the Kelly incident, Trump boycotted the next Fox News presidential debate. Again, the coverage of this decision was presented by a liberal media that had no interest in Trump's candidacy at all. It was more about the fact that he was slighting a media outlet than the integrity of what he was saying. The media made it about them instead of us. They wanted us to see this as his final moment of political suicide until we saw the polling released following the debate.

Trump won this debate without even attending. He effectively said that "if you're going to make the debate about trashing me, I won't attend" and your ratings will suffer. As a result, the remaining presidential Republican primary debates were more subdued in terms of 'gotcha questions' targeted at Trump. The questions existed but not in such an egregious fashion as with Kelly in the first Fox News debate.

Trump effectively calculated that the networks needed his presence at the debate for massive ratings and revenue boosts. He also knew that they would subjugate their political hatred of him in favor of ratings and money.

Moreover, he made it very clear that he would not and did not have to participate in customary events surrounding a viable presidential candidate because he was 'breaking the rules and getting away with it.'

He broke the rules and got away with just as we discussed in chapter 20. Instead of this being the end of his campaign, it gave him another boost.

"I could shoot someone on Fifth Avenue"

 As a result of all of the attacks by the media and the political class against Trump, the most shocking aspect of the 2016 presidential race was the fact that Trump 'broke so many of the rules and got away with it.' Seemingly no one could understand how this was possible.

 I refer you to chapter 20 for the full explanation of why the American people prefer transparency and truth over a political puppet and a fraud. You could be vehemently opposed to everything Trump represents, but to deny this reality would be to miss opportunities in your own life for success and prosperity.

 Trump made a hyperbolic comment at a campaign rally as follows:

"You know what else they say about my people? The polls, they say I have the most loyal people. Did you ever see that? Where I could stand in the middle of Fifth Avenue and shoot somebody and I wouldn't lose any voters, okay? It's like incredible," Trump said.

Many saw this comment as being narcissistic and arrogant. Perhaps in order to make my greater point I should just agree that it was those things.

However, the comment was rooted in the spirit of giving a complement to his millions of extremely loyal supporters. The comment was less about him and more about the intensity of his loyal support and following. This comment is another example of where the mainstream media and the political class judged Trump through the lens of their legalistic and arbitrary rules. It was hyperbole. His supporters saw it, but again the media was so desperate to convince you they were right about Trump, they kept doing the exact opposite unwittingly, unknowingly, and unintentionally.

The media and the experts missed the fact that most politicians are judged through a political lens and rules because we are all aware of the fact that they are disingenuous and are a puppet of their donors and handlers. We judge them by the rules they put forth because we view them as all the same: willing to lie to win an election.

Trump was different. He was willing to win the election by telling the truth. My observation here is a direct contrast to what many think about

Trump. Many Trump haters believe he told countless lies throughout the election cycle. I'm not talking about policy and procedure – he may have erred on many of those subjects. I will give them that point in order to make mine.

Trump was truthful in that he always told the American people exactly what he was thinking and what he believed. That was his biggest asset and his biggest media problem. Most politicians hide statements on policy opinions that pollsters tell them are not popular. Trump did anything but.

This is a valuable lesson for you. When you consistently tell people the truth, even when it doesn't seem to be advantageous to you, they will believe you when you make your closing arguments. If you are a lying politician who 'lies through your teeth' most of the time, your closing argument is seen as just another lie and leaves you with no control of the outcome or your own destiny.

He connected to a simple fact of human interaction. Most people will despise those things about you that completely contrast with their beliefs. But, over time they will respect you because they know they can count on and believe in what you say. There is nothing more valuable than being able to trust that someone else is telling me exactly what they believe and how they feel even if I completely disagree with it.

Most people lie or, at best, don't reveal their true beliefs out of fear of the reaction it may attract. The fact that Trump did exactly what most politicians don't do, at a desperate time in American history, is precisely why his supporters were so loyal that he could "shoot someone on Fifth Avenue and still not lose any support."

If you can't get past this comment, just remember, it's hyperbole. He doesn't actually believe he could get away with murder. It's simply a way of accentuating powerful point. Stop taking everything in life so literally.

People who support Trump take him seriously, but not literally.

"Lyin' Ted - "Bible up High…."

Another extremely formidable opponent of Trump during the 2016 Republican presidential primaries was Texas Senator Ted Cruz. Cruz was thought of as a dependable and loyal conservative who was a certain bet in a tough fight for those values.

Cruz had a style problem that caused some people not to believe him at times. I've even questioned him myself. In the end, my decision on primary election day in Georgia would come down to Trump or Cruz. As I was driving to the polls, I still didn't know for sure which one I would support. Honestly, I supported both virtually equally.

Part of my confusion arose from the way I cover primary politics on my radio program. I've made it a long-standing policy not to take sides in a primary. It's not my job to tell my audience whom I think they should choose in the voting booth. As I see it, it's my job to make sure you understand the candidates' pros and cons regardless of my personal, final decision, especially when it's a primary of conservatives. In carrying out this role, I literally had not had the occasion to determine which of the two most reflected my values and wishes for the future of America.

I'll tell you how I made my decision in the last chapter of the book.

Facing the most formal challenge yet, late in the primaries, Trump had one last opponent to defeat. Cruz and Trump had made it through 2015 and the first third of 2016 without uttering hardly a negative word against each other. In fact, it looked like running mates in the making.

This was a wise decision by both of them because each of them were so strong in their own right, that an early fight between them could have destroyed both candidates, paving the path for Marco Rubio or Jeb Bush to re-energize their campaigns and win the nomination.

What had become America's most popular reality television show, the primary election debates, demanded Cruz and Trump to have a 'falling out.' After having single-handedly eliminated almost all other competitors, the Cruz-Trump fireworks began.

There were numerous attacks on each other which would include attacks on Trump's questionable business record and failed casinos by Cruz. Trump, the master brander, coined the phrase 'Lying Ted.' Trump began preying on Cruz's perception problem I mentioned a moment ago.

I would describe it as "something is missing here but I just can't figure out." Even Cruz supporters would worry about this perception problem, but chose to support him knowing his reliable conservative positions. I later determined that it was the fact Cruz was such a great lawyer that he sometimes forgot to simply connect with people. By the time I realized this, I was hoping he was the Supreme Court nominee and Trump was the president-elect.

"Bible up high…then he lies…" became a popular Trump phrase before he would blast 'Lying Ted.' Given that the viability of Republican presidential contenders, at this point, was down to just the two of them, Trump was no longer diluted by multiple candidates attacking him as he made his closing argument. He only had to defeat Cruz, and he did so by a landslide.

Feeling pressure from Republican circles, Indiana Governor Mike Pence endorsed Cruz. Pence was a popular governor and a strong conservative. Trump's rebranding of Cruz prevailed over the endorsement of Pence and others.

Trump won the Indiana primary in a landslide by 17 percentage points earning all 57 Indiana delegates for the Republican convention. Trump had sealed the nomination even though the Republican establishment and media elites were unaware.

When I saw the results of the Indiana primary, I knew Trump was not only going to be the nominee, but would handily defeat Hillary Clinton. A Democrat with negative polling as high as Clinton's could not possibly defeat a presidential candidate like Trump with such a grassroots support. I would sound crazy for beginning to make that argument. I'll rest my case on the results of November 8, 2016.

I had already developed my 'Closet Trumpers Theory' at this point and knew there were at least 10 million voters favoring Trump that would never be reflected in the polls. These were people who had never voted in their lives or hadn't voted in decades because they were disgusted and disenfranchised by the frauds that had polluted our political process in America.

Attacking a Gold Star Family

A Gold Star family is perhaps one of the most cherished classes of American patriots. After all, these families have suffered the greatest possible sacrifice in the never-ending effort to protect our freedoms and our republic.

Captain Humayum Khan was killed in Iraq by a car bomb while protecting his detail in 2004. His parents Mr. and Mrs. Khizr Kahn appeared at the Democratic National Convention in July 2016. Khizr Kahn decried Trump's style, comments about Muslim nations, and his immigration policies as being unconstitutional and un-American.

He gave a speech that seemed overwhelmingly similar to the talking points of the Clinton campaign. It was so similar that it appeared to be scripted by a campaign speech writer. At one point, he questioned if Trump had ever read the Constitution while holding a copy in the air. This was a powerful moment for Clinton and the Democrats. But, was it genuine?

Almost every political expert in the world would have advised Trump to ignore the speech and not react to it. Again, he broke the unwritten and arbitrary rules of presidential politics by questioning why Capt. Kahn's mother (Khizr's wife) said nothing during the speech. He suggested that Captain Kahn's father likely wouldn't allow her to speak in an effort to shed light on how many immigrants from Muslim nations bring tenets of sharia law into our country, especially regarding the mistreatment and diminishment of women. The media and political class were outraged.

Another unspoken and arbitrary rule of society was revealed: "Regardless of what a Gold Star father or mother say or do, we cannot challenge their way of thinking." Apparently, 'the rules' state that these people are off-limits.

I found these assertions to be arrogant and shocking given the fact that Khan was an active immigration attorney who stood to realize financial benefit from Clinton policies and detriment by Trump policies. Does this fact not matter when it comes to putting someone's comments in context? Is it wise to let that just go unnoticed?

Why are certain people allowed to attack others in an unprovoked fashion and be unaccountable to their comments while they use their fallen son as a political shield? I wasn't alone in asking this question.

This incident sparked a debate that highlighted the fact that a number of people use their service to our country and tragedies to shield them from being questioned for their true agendas. Trump made this readily apparent.

The expert political opinion was that there was no way Trump could recover from this moment because many of his supporters were patriotic veterans and would not tolerate such commentary about a fallen soldier's family. To their surprise, many veterans recognized exactly what I just said.

They saw someone using the death of a family member as political cover for their own self-aggrandizement and profiteering.

In the end, enough Americans believed Trump, in that, the mother was not allowed to speak and that Sharia law played a part in this Gold Star dad's belief system. We further discovered that he was financially profiting from Clinton style policy to the detriment of America.

Trump's transparency and willingness to "break the rules and get away with it" prevailed here as well.

There are dozens of examples that I could share in this chapter about Trump breaking 'the rules,' suffering an immediate dip in the polls followed by an increase to a higher high once the true realities of the controversy had time to develop. This shows that speaking your mind and being honest and transparent is the best way to sustain support and respect that is unwavering. It doesn't necessarily allow you to actually shoot someone on Fifth Avenue and get away with it, but it comes damn close. The reason it comes close is because people know where your heart really is and they're able to look past your many flaws and shortcomings to find the greater good because they believe you and in you.

When you allow others to tell you how to think, behave and with what style to use, it quickly becomes obvious that you're hiding something. On that suspicion, you are then judged the same as everyone else. Trump was overwhelmingly judged, especially by his supporters, by a different set of standards given to the few who are real and honest about who they really are.

You may not like Trump's style or demeanor, and you don't have to, but for your own success and prosperity I want you to understand how an element of that style and demeanor can help you find the 'Trump in You.' You don't need to be like Trump. You just need to understand that some elements of his style can prove advantageous, so that you can have the kind of success you desire in everything that you do.

People who are easily offended by someone like Trump, if they're honest with themselves, will find that it's deeply rooted in the fact they loathe his ability to be real while they cannot. After all, they are following all of the rules society sets for behavior instead of simply being themselves.

CHAPTER TWENTY-TWO
Knowing What You Don't Know

One of the most important tenets of success is knowing what you don't know. After eliminating 17 Republican primary opponents, Trump faced a challenge he was not prepared to win.

He had actually had to earn all of the delegates he had won, again, at the Republican National Convention. There was significant risk that appointed delegates would vote for Ted Cruz or even another candidate like former nominee Mitt Romney at the convention, effectively stripping Trump of his victory.

The battle for the nomination was so hard-fought that the carnage would have to be overcome in order to even receive the nomination.

The Bush family was incredibly upset after the 'low-energy Jeb' mantra destroyed his campaign. 'Lying Ted' was still upset specifically about comments Trump had made about his father and wife. Marco Rubio was embarrassed, having admitted that his children had been disappointed that his behavior was unlike the father they knew. Rubio was also upset at Trump's backlash against him. The list of aggrieved Republicans was enormous and each of the afflicted individuals had millions of supporters. Most were unwilling to bury the hatchet and endorse Trump. This was going to be an uphill battle.

As an aside, I must add that I chuckle at the fact that these 'upset' individuals were the ones who first attacked Trump out of desperation for victory. You never play someone else's game against them or you lose every time. This observation alone was enough to sway millions of voters in Trump's favor because they knew he was a fighter and a winner. Rubio, Cruz, Bush, and many others were simply defeated and needed time to overcome their battle scars.

Notwithstanding this, Trump still could be defeated in the convention. There was enough establishment support to make it happen. Enter Paul Manafort.

Manafort was a political operative with four decades of presidential, political experience who understood intimately how to prevail in the Republican delegate process during the convention.

Trump's campaign was so impressive because it had fewer than 100 paid staffers, minimal campaign funding, and had defeated hundreds of millions of dollars' worth of established political funding and prowess held by his opponents. He was about to face a challenger in Hillary Clinton who would have over $1 billion in funding and nearly 1,000 paid staffers. More on this in chapter 24.

This was going to be a huge challenge for Trump, but he knew he had an even more significant one in the coming delegates battle at the convention.

Manafort was everything Trump's campaign was not. He was from the establishment, deeply rooted in Washington political circles, and anything but an outsider. Hiring Manafort was a humbling moment for Trump because he had to recognize his political inexperience could be his defeat if he didn't take swift action.

Manafort had joined the campaign in March 2016 and would soon become chairman. Manafort navigated Trump to a nearly uneventful victory at the Republican National Convention. The fear of delegates fleeing Trump seemed to be only a hysteria not rooted in any reality. Because of Manafort, it was. Without him, it would have been much worse for Trump.

Most people become paralyzed by the swift changes they realize they need to make and worried about outside perception. I was guilty of this in running my own company. There were many times that I needed to fire an employee or manager but was afraid of what might happen with people in my company who held a strong relationship with them. Instead, I subjugated the potential for success into worry about changes.

These moments cost me hundreds of thousands of dollars and maybe even millions in lost or potential revenue. Trump knew better.

When Corey Lewandowski, his campaign manager from the primaries was fired, and Manafort was hired, the mainstream media and political elites gave a predictable reaction: "this is the moment we knew would come where Trump's campaign begins to unravel. His political inexperience is catching up to him."

Perhaps that was true but it was dismissive of the fact that Trump realized what he didn't know. There's a business phrase. 'knowing what you don't know' is not something you would ever hear in the circles of government, politics, or bureaucracy. The perception of those individuals is that "we know everything and we certainly know what's best." In unfettered arrogance, they lack the humility to concern themselves with accountability or admission of weakness. This is one of the reasons Trump was so successful.

There was no way to dispute Trump's decades of success. Many would argue his casino bankruptcies are the 'smoking gun proof' we need that he is a fraud, a phony, and a failure. What most people realize is that that every successful businessman has failures. Many also realized that Trump was only a minority owner at the time of those casino bankruptcies and that he was mainly receiving royalties for the use of his name. This hardly pointed to failure but instead brilliance.

Hiring Manafort would be an example of the type of humility for which Trump is never given credit. He knew he had a severe weakness and he saw the appropriate person to fill that void. Trump had no idea how to compete in the very legalistic delegate process of the Republican National Convention. Manafort did.

It's in these moments that we also frequently make some of our biggest mistakes. Because we become dependent upon other people for things we cannot do well, we frequently align ourselves with people who may present a host of unintended consequences. We have to calculate these risks each and every time.

In retrospect, I'm certain that Trump would not hire Manafort again. After all, it's Manafort's Ukraine and Russia connections that were used by operatives in the FBI and our intelligence community to spy on the Trump campaign and discover several interactions with Russian officials. It's because of this that Trump's first year as president has been mired in a Russian collusion investigation with former FBI director, now special counsel Robert Mueller.

As I write this book, Manafort is facing three rounds of serious charges that include money laundering, tax-evasion, wire-fraud, and not registering as a foreign agent. It's unclear as to why Manafort was fired in August 2016 after handily delivering Trump the victory at the convention he was hired to ensure. One has to imagine that Trump may have become increasingly concerned about Manafort's shadiness and found him of little value as a campaign manager after serving his intended purpose.

Had Trump not hired Manafort, he may have survived the convention. Because Trump hired

Manafort, he created a massive legal problem that has clouded his first year in office. I doubt he is second guessing these decisions. Most successful people don't.

What Trump did, instead, was recognize he needed yet another change during the critical last moments of his campaign. He didn't allow the likely political fallout of such a change to delay his action. Perhaps his best hire ever in his business and newfound political career was Kellyann Conway. She was an insider where she needed to be but also unique in possessing an outsider style. Many were shocked that she agreed to work as Trump's new campaign manager. After all, she was well-known in the circles of Washington D.C. Trump knew Conway had everything he was missing. She had the political connections and prowess of campaign management to outsmart Clinton's campaign. Trump chose Conway because she understood the political operation of his opponent, Clinton, well enough to help them message against it.

Conway was a strong enough individual, with enough humility, that she didn't need to be the puppet master as she might be in a typical political campaign. Trump not only chose someone who was highly qualified, but also had the right demeanor to serve Trump.

A typical campaign manager coalesces the advice, research, and opinions of top political advisers in order to instruct the candidate as to how to frame and position their policies and messages in interviews and speeches. While a candidate has significant editorial influence over all of it, many of them become a mere puppet of the political elites they hire. This was not the case with Trump, even after hiring Conway.

Trump surrounded himself with people who both challenged him but also agreed with his approach and style. In chapter 18, "Dealing with the Naysayers," by explaining the importance of getting negative and defeatist minds out of your life, I also explained the importance of having people around you that would challenge you.

Trump's campaign involved a significant number of people who would challenge his efforts through a political lens but would support him in whatever he decided to do. They believed in him as a whole. This is the perfect blend of having people who support you without surrounding yourself with apathetic "yes-men." We all know that we need to hear where our positions or approaches may be wrong, but once we make a decision, we want those in our inner circle to support it and wish us success.

Trump's campaign, regardless of what you've heard, did not have naysayers or "yes-men." It's true the Trump did have people that show him positive news articles. This can appear to be a "yes-man" behavior, but it's important to note that we need to also focus on the things that are working best for us and expand on them.

The key to success for any person, regardless of your style, demeanor, or approach is knowing what you don't know and always questioning where you could be wrong. If you'll take this message "Where could I be wrong?" and post it on the wall in front of your desk, it will transform your career and your life. It will bring you peace you cannot imagine because it will reduce your strife and align your expectations with reality.

It will help you identify weaknesses and find partners to fill those voids. We are born with special talents and skills. We shouldn't spend most of our time trying to improve our weaknesses. We will always be frustrated by the limits of our weaknesses. Instead, we should focus on expanding our strengths. People like Trump always do this. There is no limit to how strong you can become when you focus on improving upon your natural talents.

 In terms of our weaknesses, 'there are people for that!'

CHAPTER TWENTY-THREE
Winning with Less

In the previous chapter, I mentioned the difference in the campaign staffing size between Clinton and Trump. Trump, at the peak of his general election campaign, had approximately 100 paid staffers. Clinton had nearly 1,000. This meant she was burning through cash at an alarming rate while Trump was spending his own money.

If this fact alone doesn't draw the sharp contrast between Clinton and Trump, nothing else will. Trump accomplished with a tenth of the resources what Clinton couldn't accomplish with ten times the cash. Less is frequently more especially when the goal is winning.

One of the biggest issues weighing on voters during the 2016 election was the role government now played in our lives. This was especially the case in the wake of eight years of the President Obama bureaucracy. To those in the financial industry, the Dodd-Frank legislation had been a devastating blow, making life hell and their job nearly impossible. The IRS had been weaponized against some conservative, political action committees. We had yet to learn this in 2016, but corruption had even penetrated the preeminent law-enforcement division of country, the FBI.

 One of the reasons for this is that the government believes more is more. If there's a problem with schools, we have to spend more money. If there's a problem with crime, we have to hire more cops. If an agency needs to expand, we have to build a bigger building. Government never thinks about using existing space and reducing the size of cubicles or offices. It never thinks of combining resources from multiple departments to accomplish exponential goals. It also never thinks about cutting costs in one area to expend those resources where they are even more urgently needed. In other words, government has no idea how businesses actually operate. I find this shocking given that The US government is the largest 'business' with the most sizable budget in the world.

 By contrast, business leaders will always strive to maintain their margins no matter what threats or circumstances are placed on them. Businesses live and die by their margins. This means, as technology increases and we live in a more digital world, we must always strive to determine how we can create more productivity and value with less manpower. This means we can only focus on initiatives that actually work and on issues that matter.

 Trump determined that his campaign was blessed to be followed by a very loyal set of supporters who felt forgotten by America's political process. He determined that these were people that were unlikely to vote unless they felt the candidate was significantly different, as he was. In the wake of the election, these people were disparagingly called the "Cracker Barrel crowd." I wrote about this in a Townhall.com article following the election.

Here is part of what I wrote:
MSNBC was proud to report that Trump won 76% of the counties with a Cracker Barrel and 22% of the counties with a Whole Foods grocery store. This is code for "the dumb people in America voted for Trump and us smart people get a pass for being wrong.

"To infer that the 'Cracker Barrel crowd' is any less relevant to our country is no different than asserting someone has less relevance because of their race, religion or national origin. It's bigoted and it should not be indulged. I'm not offended by it and I'm certainly not angry like many of the petulant children who we've seen rioting and

protesting in the streets because they don't like the outcome of our democratic process.

I know the 'Cracker Barrel crowd.' It's called "my family." I grew up in middle Tennessee working for the company that manufactures all the rocking chairs at the Cracker Barrel's across America. In fact, it was my first job and it was the hardest work I've ever done.

On any given day, many of my close and extended family may eat at Cracker Barrel. They are what we call 'the silent majority.' They go to church on Sunday, they save for retirement, they teach their kids morals/values and they give to charity. They don't like confrontation or conflict and they rarely like discussing politics (with outsiders) because they don't want extra strife in their life. They want to live humbly and peacefully in a free nation and enjoy their life without extensive government or outside interference.

They are disgusted by the direction of this nation. They don't hate anyone and they certainly don't feel that they are 'better' than anyone else.

I'm part of the 'Whole Foods crowd' now. I've been blessed in success and I love to eat healthy. But, my roots are still in the country on a farm at the 'Cracker Barrel.' And, I'm not ashamed of it.

It's in that environment where I find the most peace.

Trump effectively realized that a certain percentage of the country would vote Republican as a default. He realized that approximately 40% of the country would never vote for him. In his typical business acumen, he assessed that what remained was about 20-30% of the country. He had to convince that group to support him AND show up at the polls on Election Day. This crowd was comprised of a large faction of people who despised Hillary Clinton and didn't much like Trump. It was also a group of people who liked him but typically never vote. His focus became the latter. He won most of the latter and even some of the former.

 His online marketing, with a significantly smaller budget than Clinton's, was targeted at the 'Cracker Barrel Crowd.' His rallies, speeches, and events all occurred in areas that would appeal to these people. His staff stayed ultra-concentrated on this group. It was nearly impossible to land a Trump interview in markets like Atlanta where I host my show. Yet, small town radio hosts in Iowa, Wisconsin, and South Carolina would easily get repeated opportunities to interview Trump. They were in markets full of Cracker Barrels!

His campaign understood that Trump support fully outpaced Clinton's, IF they would show up to vote.

The moral to this story is simple: the shotgun approach to marketing is expensive and labor intensive. The rifle approach only takes one laser focused shot to hit the target.

When I moved to Atlanta, the main reason was to grow my media career. However, our real estate business was incredibly important as a bridge for our future. Atlanta's total extended metro population is over six million people. As a media market, it's nearly five million people. It's extremely expensive to reach full penetration and grow name-recognition with every consumer in a city this size. I also determined that my political opinions and commentary would be a turnoff to roughly half of the market. So, why spend money to reach the entire market when you've already lost half of it due to your style?

At the time, I didn't feel like I was copying Trump. I knew nothing about his coming political aspirations. I was just simply doing what it takes to succeed without first going bankrupt attempting to figure it out. Clinton went politically bankrupt trying to figure out how to be everything to everyone.

The typical advice of most 'experts' is "you can't run a service business while spouting all these political opinions. You'll destroy your business!"

They would advise that you have to choose one. "Pick between real estate or media because you can't be political and be successful in real estate" (or any business for that matter) to which I would respond "bull shit!"

This represents a small-minded and defeatist mentality. I decided to take Trump's laser focused campaign approach, which hadn't even occurred in 2014 when this started for us, to reduce the size of Atlanta to a tenth of the total population: 600,000. In Charleston, I had effectively marketed to the entire community of roughly the same number of people. It wasn't that expensive and real estate prices in Charleston were even more expensive than Atlanta - netting more commission per sale. If only I had been forced to reduce my market to a specific audience, I would have made more money and profit back then.

I spent thousands of dollars acquiring legitimate research showing where conservative voters with upper-middle-class incomes lived in Atlanta. I looked at their voting histories from 2008 to 2014, their income demographics, and their proximity to my office. I then created a digital geo-fence around those areas which reduced the market size to just over one million people. I still had a problem. There were a lot of liberal people within that geo-fence that still would want nothing to do with my business or beliefs.

I had to find a way to further isolate the potential customer base. Given my experience in radio, I knew that people who followed local conservative radio stations or national hosts like Rush Limbaugh or Sean Hannity were more likely to be conservative. They would be more likely to enjoy my commentary. In other words, I needed to be attracting customers to my business brand who would not be offended by my media brand. No Crabtree "snowflakes" for me! This isolated my list down to about 600,000 people.

In our first year of Atlanta real estate sales, we sold as much as our prior year as top five agents in Charleston. Obviously our market share wasn't that high in Atlanta because there are 50,000 agents here. However, I could care less about rank, because, in business, it's about revenue.

Without spending a billion of his own fortune, Trump spent approximately a tenth of what the last two presidents did in order to win the election. He did it by applying business acumen and targeted marketing to connect his message with the people he needed to defeat his opponent.

Without a doubt, finding the 'Trump in You' requires you to do the same unless you want to blow your hard earned money trying to figure it out the hard way.

A key objective to success in politics, business, or any organization is to determine how to do more with less. Since the financial crisis I have learned a valuable lesson. Businesses should always seek to reduce the costs of acquiring customers and increase its reputation until it becomes apparent that those cost reductions have affected profit.

This means gradually reducing the cost components even if some are working until you find the critical, tipping point where reducing it further will cost you revenue and profit. Focusing on this is far more important than the bureaucracy and red tape most businesses are constantly consumed with handling.

Remember, it's better to be respected by colleagues, friends, and neighbors than just liked. When people overwhelming like you without first respecting you, this usually means you have allowed them to control you and set the tone for your life. They may be happy, but it's very hard for you to be. Your happiness and strength come first. You can't be a force for good for the world around you if you are in shambles as a person.

Your health, strength, and prosperity must take center stage, so you can share it with the world.

I'm reminded of the safety presentation at the beginning of each commercial airline flight. The head flight attendant states:

"In the event of a loss in cabin pressure, an oxygen mask will fall from the ceiling. To start the flow of oxygen, pull the mask towards you. Place it firmly over your nose and mouth, secure the elastic band behind your head, and breathe normally. Although the bag does not inflate, oxygen is flowing to the mask. If you are traveling with a child or someone who requires assistance, secure your mask on first, and then assist the other person."

These are very selfish instructions. Basically the message is to save your life first and then worry about other people. Losers would interpret it that way. Winners understand that if we first strengthen ourselves, we can then be a much greater force for helping others around us.

It's this same level of self-awareness that is needed in your business and personal life to understand that adding more costs, people, offices, and stuff does not add value. Always striving to be a sharper, smarter, and better version of yourself and your business is what is most important.

Stay focused on what matters. You don't need 'more' to accomplish your goals, you may need 'less' so you can remain more focused on what really works.

CHAPTER TWENTY-FOUR
Curiosity

A lot of Americans aren't curious. They live in their own world surrounding by a protective, emotional cocoon unwilling to intellectually explore anything. Many people are vehemently afraid to discover information or details that may conflict with their world-view or values.

By contrast, most exceptional business leaders like Trump are curious. They are curious about different cultures, different viewpoints, people, science, technology, and a host of interesting things that cross their paths daily. They connect to people instantly by being inquisitive about who they are, their journey, and their unique talents.

One of the best ways to build trust and earn respect is to listen. Listening is a form of curiosity. Have you ever noticed that you are more endeared to people who listen to all of what you have to say? Imagine if you listened to other people and attempt to be interested in who they are, how they think, and what they have to say? You'll find that earning their trust and respect is far easier when you do that. No amount of 'sales pitch' can be as effective in building trust in relationships than being curious and listening to other people's stories. When you hear them, you can respond to them with solutions and details about what really matters to them.

Trump's preparation for his candidacy was all about listening. A top campaign official described his first days of preparation as listening to talk radio. He wasn't listening to hosts like me, he was listening to the callers. These were the forgotten people who call radio stations, use a fake name, and transparently express their greatest fears and concerns for our country. Trump knew this was invaluable insight into winning over the voters that had refused to support former Republican candidates like John McCain and Mitt Romney.

He listened and he listened, for a year. As a result, he made some of the most common themes and worries of these average American callers his primary campaign initiatives: immigration, security, ISIS, government corruption, and excessive regulations to name a few.

He was curious about the reasons behind why people were so concerned about their country. He repeatedly tapped into their hearts and minds by repurposing those messages and illustrating to them that he had heard them. You can decry this as manipulation if you wish. However, I would simply call it listening and acting accordingly. Earning trust and respect is less about convincing people you are one of them and more about convincing others that you hear them and will respond to their needs.

I had a closing ratio (appointment success rate) in the real estate business of over 90%. In other words, when I went to a listing appointment, I would almost always be awarded the listing on the home in the face of any amount of competition. What was the secret to this?

I simply listened to the home seller. I knew my competition and presented specific reasons why I was a better choice to serve their interests than my competitors.

I was always curious about people, their lives, and their careers. I found it both helpful and fascinating to understand why they were selling/ moving and what they did for a living. Many of my associates and colleagues could never understand why I would sometimes spend two to three hours at a listing presentation in an industry where 45 minutes was average. They thought I was wasting my time.

First, I wasn't boring. I could keep the seller entertained and wanting more information. But, I also found every new experience extremely educational as I learned about various industries, life struggles, and family dilemmas that I would be a part of helping solve through their home sale.

I was legitimately curious about their lives, motivations, and causes and thus they would spend far longer with me than most people because I allowed them to share in a way most real estate agents would simply avoid in the interest of moving on to the next sales opportunity.

 I wasn't being fake. I was simply interested and curious. I was also making sure that I wanted to get involved with these people. After two to three hours, I would sometimes conclude that this relationship would be a nightmare. I had a clever way of encouraging those people to choose my competitor.

 They never suspected I was interviewing them as much as they were me. I realized at an early age that a bad client who would 'suck my emotions dry' was far more expensive to my career than any commission they could pay. Because I listened so much at thousands of meetings over two decades, I became very adept at determining who was a good fit for my business and who was not.

 Because I spent so much 'up-front time' being curious about my clients, I could also effectively frame each decision in our client-agent relationship with "how this would move [them] toward or away from their goals." This made connecting to their decision-making process much easier and my style incredibly more effective. When a real estate agent spends most of their time attempting to convince their clients that they can be trusted, your service level declines and so does your income. Building trust is most easily accomplished through listening and reflecting that person's own statements back to them with your own style.

 Throughout my career, I remember the feeling of believing most of my clients trusted me so strongly, that I could have taken advantage of them on many levels. I never did. The main reason I didn't is because I didn't believe in 'blood money.' 'Blood money' is money derived from criminal activity in most cases. In business, I saw it as forcing someone to do something they don't wish to do (fighting against natural inclination). It's also hard for me to sleep at night when I've taken advantage of someone else's disaster, especially if I created it. I simply don't believe in that.

 I've sold hundreds of millions of dollars of real estate by simply listening more than my competition. Certainly, my media work in tandem with my real estate career was a huge advantage. But, my closing technique was simply being curious and listening.

Trump listened to the people he needed (remember my closet Trumpers Theory?) to actually go to the polls and deliver him victory. He spoke to them at each opportunity and ignored the political class of experts and media pundits who called his approach laughable and untenable.

While most people were unwilling to listen to Trump, he was listening and reacting mostly to the ones that mattered most. Being curious isn't natural for most people, but you better learn how to expand your general curiosity of other people and their lives because you need these allies on your journey toward purpose and success.

My son recently told me that he sometimes feels dumb because he asks so many questions. I may be guilty of causing this feeling a bit because I've been known to tell him, "you've reached your 1,000 question limit for today." I'm somewhat joking when I say that, but he does tend to overwhelm, even me, with questions. When he brought this feeling to my attention, I told him that asking questions is one of the most important things you can do to learn. I looked at him and said, "You'll be very successful because you are a lot like me. You are curious about everything and you want to understand how things work. Never let anyone tell you that asking questions is a sign of lacking intelligence, annoying, or wrong. "

Until you reach the point where people frequently say to you, "you ask too many questions," you have room for growth in this area.

Start being curious today about other people, their careers, and different industries and explore ideas and values that compete with yours. If you disagree, instead of attempting to change their hearts and minds, attempt to understand how they developed that opinion or belief.

Ask these questions:

How did you first starting believing that or thinking that way?

At what point in your life did you first begin believing that?

Explain to me what leads you to that conclusion?

This is a better way to both challenge and understand something that contrasts with your way of thinking. You'll also find that this approach allows you to remain close and allied with people for whom you may disagree. Creating enemies for no reason is not what this book suggests.

If you believe someone is lying about a belief or conviction, there is usually a very simply way to find out. Ask them what happened in their life that first led them to this way of thinking or belief). If they can't identify the 'flash-point' that changed their thinking or developed their belief, they likely are just parroting someone else, saying what they think is 'cool,' or lying.

I love the phrase, "God gave you two ears and one mouth. Use them in that proportion." Not only is that factually true, it's a general secret to overall success.

CHAPTER TWENTY-FIVE
Conclusion: Why I Voted for Trump

The reason I'm explaining my vote is that it has much more to do with Trump's style, demeanor, and business acumen than it does politics. You'll understand shortly.

On March 1st, 2016, I was driving to the voting booth at my kid's elementary school, undecided. I really liked Marco Rubio, but I felt he wasn't ready. Just like President Obama, he needed more experience before he took the helm of the most powerful executive seat in the world.

Ohio Governor John Kasich lost me. He struck me as sanctimonious, arrogant, and not believable. He was too busy rattling off his resume of qualifications in order to appeal to voters like me instead of telling me his vision for America.

Unless I wanted to waste my vote, that left Senator Cruz and Donald J. Trump. I had always liked Cruz for his policy positions and his tough stances in Washington. I also saw it as a badge of honor that he wasn't well liked in the halls of Congress. But, was he strong enough to give this country a dose of what it really needed right now?

I was conflicted. I felt that I knew exactly what a Cruz presidency would look like and knew that

I'd very much agree with most of his actions and positions. With Trump, I just knew it would be transformative but had no idea how he would really govern.

 As I was standing in the voting booth, I was conflicted, then a thought hit me. It was the catalyst for this book. "Trump is just a more bombastic and accomplished version of me," I thought. "If I vote against Trump, it would be like voting against myself." Most of the concern and fear that had been projected on Trump's candidacy was nothing more than the backlash I had personally experienced for the last two decades as I took on my industry and served as a consumer advocate.

 Without hesitation, I pushed the button for "Donald John Trump."

 I made the calculation that many people made: He's got all the fame and money he could want. It's probably not that. He's a businessman so it's believable that he'll lean conservative. He's nailed nearly 20 Republicans so he definitely knows how to win. If I'm wrong, the worst thing that can happen is that Republicans (and the entire political system) will be shocked into change.

 I knew that change was desperately needed, and I had no doubt he would provide it. If Trump failed,

I thought, it wouldn't be any worse than Clinton. If he succeeded, it may be studied a century from now as the flash-point when the country was spiraling out of control and was saved by the 45th president. I saw very little downside compared to the status quo and a whole lot of potential.

 People that know me well have told me, "you are better than being a Trump supporter, Bryan. I know you too well. There is no way you can really support this man…" Maybe there is some truth in that statement, but not really. Maybe my standards are higher than what Trump brings in terms of style to the presidency. But, at this time, I don't care. Who am I to judge who is better than the other? I simply know we need change and he's the only one on the stage that really appeared different. It wasn't a moral decision because politicians can act like they are morally superior only to be far worse than their alternative.

One of Trump's most polarizing talents is being candid and dosing his audiences with harsh reality. This is something our country desperately needs even if it's difficult to tolerate.

 This is a president that refuses to cozy up to elite Washington powers and succumb to their demands. He refuses to be beaten into submission like every president since Reagan has been. He refuses to let the media or the political experts bully him into compromising his principles or breaking his commitment to the American people. I call that integrity. You may disagree but 'integrity' is not a judgment of quality. It's simply being unwavering on your values and principles.

I don't feel we've had a president with integrity since Reagan. Reagan not only had integrity, he was a bold leader unwilling to cave to the principles of the establishment class. That also made him effective.

President Carter also had integrity. He was an honorable man both before and after his presidency, but his leadership skills were severely lacking and therefore he was unable to execute his policies effectively. Having integrity is very important to success, but it doesn't ensure it.

Trump is a disrupter and his candidacy came at a time when this country needed a significant disruption. We've become a country mired in bureaucracy, victim mentality, wealth shaming, wealth envy, and a host of other unattractive traits. This comes partly because our government has inserted itself into our challenges and problems as the most viable solution. It's not. This arrogance has penetrated deeply into the agencies and departments of our government and its over two million employees. Trump is making many of these entitled 'servants' incredibly uncomfortable.

As a result, many of them are exposing themselves as frauds or 'bad actors' as they fight back against the will of the people.

As I was completing this book, I met with a prominent real estate industry executive. I made the observation that as real estate brokerages had become larger and larger (some with thousands of agents under their brand), the propensity to mire themselves into compliance and legalistic measures had distracted them from serving their clients. Instead of teaching their agents how to sell to and service clients effectively, they were now teaching them how to have disclosures signed properly to limit liability to the real estate company itself. This is the antithesis of customer service.

The executive agreed with me. She continued, "Bryan, the government has gotten so strict about independent contractors that [we can't demand or force them to attend sales training any longer]."

Before I sold my real estate company, training was our primary focus. Every agent was required to attend mandatory sales training. We taught them how to structure sales contracts to best serve their clients' interests, how to prospect for new clients, and how to conduct presentations so their sales conversion-rate was as high as possible. We recognized that very few people enjoy sitting in a classroom, but without this invaluable knowledge we would risk providing inferior service to our clients and experiencing lackluster sales due to poor sales skills of our staff.

Because the Obama administration spent eight years weaponizing the IRS as a punitive, political operation against businesses, real estate companies can no longer require training of sales agents. They can offer it and encourage it, but they can't demand it.

In an effort to rob companies of their profits and drive more revenue to the federal government for the sake of entitlement and costly, politically driven policy, they have destroyed a safety net for the American public: education and training of real estate agents. They have encouraged top real estate companies to leave their agents less trained, more dangerous, and less accountable because if they do require training, they risk their entire business model being destroyed by the IRS.

In doing so, this shifts the focus of major real estate firms from producing quality agents and customer service and replaces it with compliance, bureaucracy, and 'red-tape.' The negative and unintended consequences of the last few decades of government actions have destroyed creativity, exploration, and risk. These traits are what built the fabric of our great nation.

This sick phenomenon exists in almost every industry and the American people see it. They simply want someone to disrupt it and fix it. Trump was the only candidate that presented any level of hope for such a disruption.

Time will tell whether or not this Trump disruption will net a positive change or not.

I know plenty of people who don't like Trump but equally dislike Hillary Clinton or similar politicians. At least with Trump, there is a chance Washington will experience change. We certainly won't rid it of its problems and corruption, but any improvement is desperately needed.

I honestly believe that the real estate industry disruption as I've described above is too far rooted into our culture to be greatly altered. I hope I'm wrong. If not, the positive aspect of such a chaotic reality is that it gives smaller companies the opportunity to take more risks because the IRS is focused so heavily on larger players wherein they can rob….uh…I mean collect the most punitive money in the end. Smaller companies face less scrutiny and therefore can walk up to the 'legal-line.' Larger firms tend to stay far away from the 'legal-line' established by the government thus limiting their competitiveness.

I wrote this book because dozens of authors have written incredible books chronicling the Trump revolution of our politics. They've explained why he won and how he won, but not what built the foundation for a person such as Trump to realize such incredible success. Hopefully, this book has shed light on that.

Moreover, my goal was to wake you up with this book, ask you to become stronger, and fight for what you most 'believe in.' You'll never realize your potential by being passive, 'professional,' 'presidential,' or any of those euphemisms that the powerful elites use to keep you in your place. Sometimes you have to kick ass and take names.

You have to find the 'Trump in You,' selectively pick your battles, and fight to win your personal war for purpose and success.

Don't allow your industry to force you into following arbitrary and unilateral unwritten rules that will derail your success. Don't worry what the industry or political 'establishment' thinks of your or your behavior. They are neither your creator nor your judge. Even with all your flaws, never allow anyone to convince you that being yourself is wrong. Work on isolating your weaknesses but don't change who you are to find approval from society as you never will. Focus on your strengths and become even stronger. It's easier to become exceptional in areas where we have natural talents.

Always maintain your integrity. On the surface this means being honest and having strong moral principles. In my definition, it means being consistent and rejecting the pressure to be a hypocrite. Always seek what's right, not what seems popular. 'Popularity' fades, but righteousness never does.

Understand that righteousness is doing what's right expecting no reward or recognition for doing so. Self-righteousness is the opposite: projecting moral superiority and doing what's right solely for the expected notoriety or monetary gain.

Be willing to challenge your own thinking. Be bold and don't listen to the naysayers and jealous crowd. The jealous will show up at the first sign of your success. Fire back at the 'Be Nice Crowd' that tries to hijack your success under the veil of professionalism. They are anything but professional. Instead they are bad actors and frauds projecting their flaws on you. Don't allow it. Don't be a doormat. These sanctimonious people are accustomed to people deferring to their self-proclaimed greatness. Do the opposite.

Be a counterpuncher to defend your reputation to set the precedent that you will not tolerate unprovoked personal attacks. Stop apologizing unless you sincerely regret your statements or actions for which an apology is demanded. This means don't question yourself just because you are being attacked by others. The attack may be in fact a justification that you are right and they are wrong. Don't assume you are always right, but don't allow others to cause you to question yourself. Allow the facts to be your guide. This means keep an open mind at all times. Be honest with yourself and trust your heart and your gut, not the words of others.

Don't hold grudges against people, even those who damaged you, but don't forget what others do. Don't be naive and allow other people to continue to hurt you. Get incompetent people out of your life or they will destroy you.

You were put on this Earth to do something much bigger than simply just what's best for you. At the same time, remember you must always secure and maintain the best reputation possible because that is a foundation for your purposes. Don't allow others to control your image. Don't get sucked into the trickery that finding some immediate success or monetary advantage is worth subjugating your image or relinquishing control to someone else regardless of how volatile your experiences may be as a result.

Be sure you always ''know what you don't know.' If you miss important facts or realities or struggle in certain areas, avoiding them will destroy your future and path to your purpose. Notwithstanding this, listen to your heart and chase your burning desires and dreams allowing no one to convince you they are wrong, stupid, or idiotic. Only you get to determine what is right or wrong for your life.

Set bold goals. What you focus on expands. If your goals and focus are tepid, your overall success and influence will be as well. I've always liked the phrase, "reach for the moon, because if you fall, you will fall amongst the stars." So many people are afraid to reach high because they are afraid to be defined by their failures. Only you can define yourself. If you allow others to define you, you will most likely fail. If you define success, in your own way, you can almost never fail.

Trump has failed more times than most Americans have in business. He's also succeeded hundreds of times because he was willing to lose in order to eventually win.

Whether you like the policies, demeanor, or general approach of our 45th president, no one can deny that the tenets of his victory as described in this book are equally available to almost every American.

You can have as much success as you want. The only barrier is your own mind. Cut out the clutter created by others and calculate the sacrifices that you are personally willing to make.

Finding 'The Trump in You' is about finding the fighter inside of yourself that society and culture says should remain hidden at all times.

Reject society and culture's limits and find the exceptional person you are a capable of being. I'm not suggesting you be like Trump. I'm suggesting you find 'The Trump in You.' This is the person you really are, without constraints, without worry of what people will think while you live the life you are capable of living - not the one everyone describes as "good enough."

Will you look back at the end of your life and say, "I wish I had done more?" Or, will you say, "my work is done!"

Does your life end with an exclamation point or a question mark?

It's your choice.

ABOUT THE AUTHOR

Bryan Crabtree

Bryan can be heard on talk radio stations throughout the country as an expert analyst of the top news stories, finance and housing in our media cycle. He is also seen on major national and international cable networks doing the same. His writing has appeared in TheHill.com, Townhall.com, DailyCaller.com, Lifezette.com and ClashDaily.com and *The Washington Times.*

He is the publisher of Talk40.com. "Talk40" is a conservative news blog hosting some of the nations' most prestigious writers and seeks to highlight the truth commonly hidden by the media in the top 40 stories of the current news cycle.

Bryan Crabtree began broadcasting at WDBL in Springfield, TN in 1993 while attending Springfield High School. After hosting an afternoon program for more than a year, he moved his radio career to Nashville's Award Winning WSIX, "The Big 98" where he produced Hollywood Nights (nominated for 1996 Country Music Association Large Market Host of the Year); While in Nashville, Crabtree simultaneously hosted a Sunday show syndicated on more than 250 Christian Radio Stations. Crabtree hosted mornings on WPZM in Hunstville, AL before moving to Memphis for Heritage WGKX as Production Director and on-air talent. He was honored with the M.A.R.S. Award in 1997 for the most creative commercial production. Crabtree later moved to Charleston, SC for the launch of WNKT and began producing for Hollywood Productions and other clients for national copy and radio imaging.

 In 2000, Bryan Crabtree began, what would become a successful real estate brokerage, while remaining in radio for Heritage Talker, WTMA in Charleston, SC; a position he held for 13 years. In May 2013, he began hosting mornings on Simulcast Talker WQSC 1340 and AM950, The Voice. Bryan most recently was the live afternoon host on Atlanta's Biz1190 from 4-6pm weekdays and airing again on AM 920 The Answer from 9-11pm.

Bryan Crabtree has provided a unique model of Writing, Speaking & Talk Radio information to the Atlanta community by inspiring greatness in his stories, speaking for the silent majority and adding common sense to common issues we face.